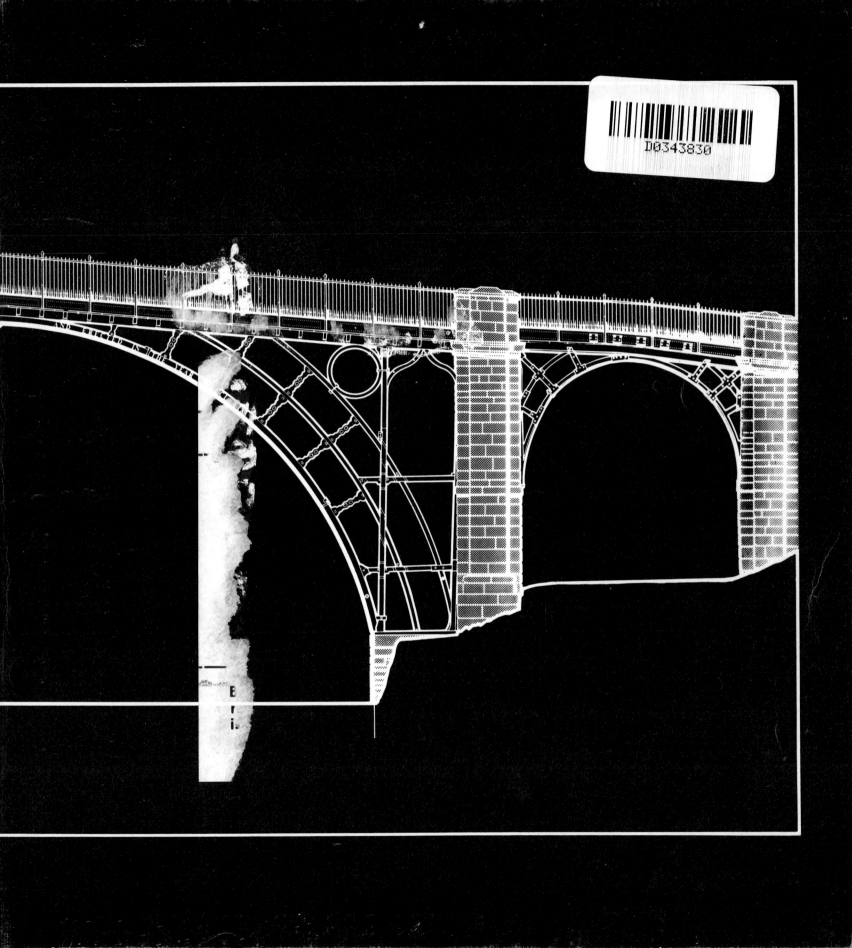

# IRONBRIDGE

# IRONBRIDGE
## Landscape of Industry

Text by NEIL COSSONS

Photographs by HARRY SOWDEN

CASSELL
LONDON

CASSELL & COMPANY LIMITED
35 Red Lion Square, London WC1R 4SG
and at Sydney, Auckland, Toronto,
Johannesburg,
an affiliate of
Macmillan Publishing Co., Inc.,
New York.

First published 1977

ISBN 0 304 29693 7

Filmset and printed in Great Britain by
BAS Printers Limited, Over Wallop,
Hampshire
F577

# Foreword

Ironbridge and Coalbrookdale were the cradle of our industrial revolution. It was here, in 1709, that Abraham Darby first smelted iron using coke; here, in the making of the Iron Bridge itself, that the revolutionary techniques of prefabrication were first fully exploited in iron.

For a few brief decades the Ironbridge flame burned bright. Then better transport and better supplies of fuel elsewhere drained much of the life from it. Still, ingenuity and fine craftsmanship in specialist manufacture kept it burning well into this century. As Neil Cossons tells us, and the poetic, atmospheric photographs of Harry Sowden so eloquently underline, the ground in these parts 'grows iron'. Iron railings, iron signposts, iron chimney-pots, even iron gravestones. And in this book we see a century and a half of crisp artistry in iron set in appealing contrast against the romantic decay of buildings and townscape that are Ironbridge today.

But stop! Beware romantic decay. It is inherently unstable. Neil Cossons knows this. As director of the Ironbridge Gorge Museum Trust, he wants to conserve as much as he can of the buildings and artefacts of the place, for their own sake and for the sake of a growing number of genuinely interested, fascinated visitors. But people also live here. They cannot be condemned to dwell in a dead museum. Happily Cossons's goal is a lively, vital one. Even so, it requires from him and all others concerned a delicate balancing act, achieving necessary improvements without falling into the errors of what he calls 'the myth of enhancement'. This beautiful book should help many more people to understand the true spirit of Ironbridge which he seeks to keep alive.

TONY ALDOUS

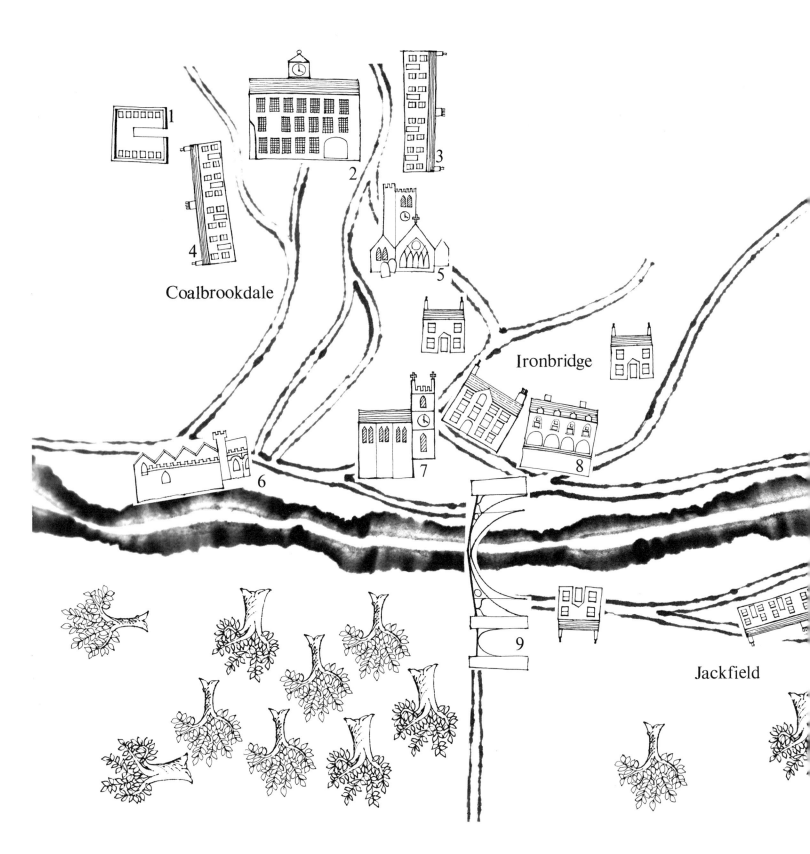

Coalbrookdale

Ironbridge

Jackfield

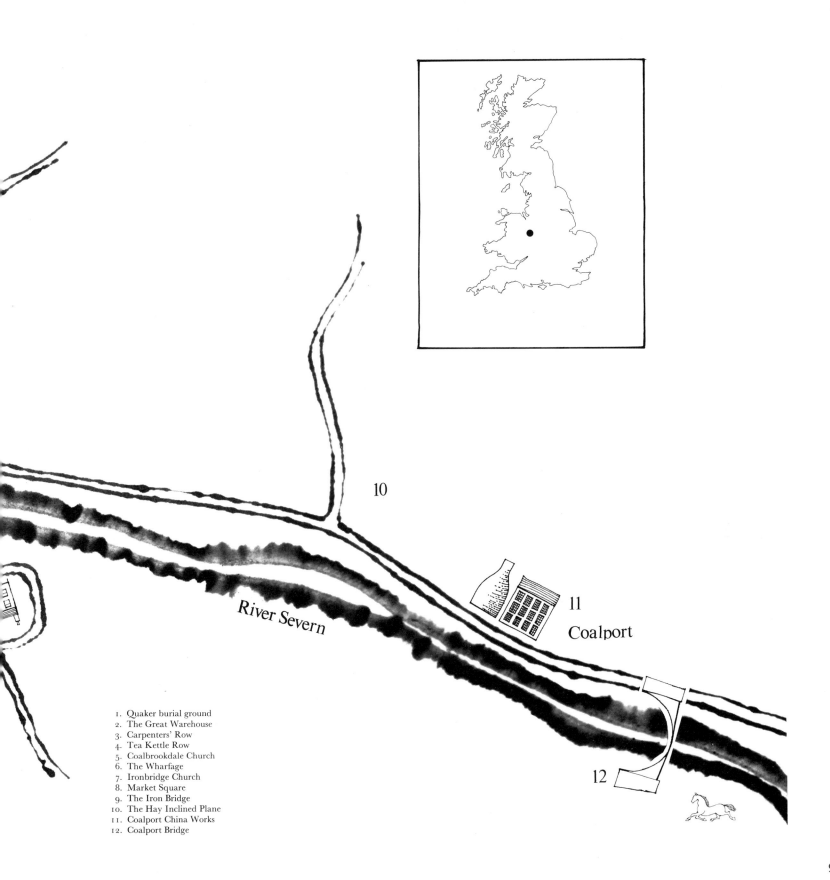

10

11 Coalport

River Severn

12

1. Quaker burial ground
2. The Great Warehouse
3. Carpenters' Row
4. Tea Kettle Row
5. Coalbrookdale Church
6. The Wharfage
7. Ironbridge Church
8. Market Square
9. The Iron Bridge
10. The Hay Inclined Plane
11. Coalport China Works
12. Coalport Bridge

The Ironbridge Gorge is an enigma, an illusion of the mind which cannot be brought into reality or into the world of today. Its importance to us derives from many things, all to do with the past, and as an amalgam of the events of the past crystallized in the present it holds a peculiar and unique fascination. It stands with ancient Egypt, Athens and Rome as a place of outstanding significance in the evolution of Man and as such demands the most thoughtful attention and detailed care. But the Gorge is much more than an archaeological monument of the Industrial Revolution, it is a place in which people live, a place of great beauty and scenic attraction and, as a result of the last half century or so of gradual decline, it is a place which wears the indefinable and transient patina of decay. Neglect and the deterioration that goes with it have contributed as much as anything to the character of the place as it is today.

This book is in part a requiem for the Gorge and for the illusion which one way or another had to disappear. Further decay would have destroyed much of it anyway, but the Gorge is being rescued for today and tomorrow and people must not live with an illusion ruling their lives. Piranesian decrepitude cannot be preserved and so for a place which over a short period of its history lived with the ultimate effects of neglect to have any future at all, rehabilitation has had to be the key word. The facts of revival are there for everyone to see and some might question the motives and philosophies lying behind much of what has been achieved. But regardless of how well or not so well the future of the Gorge is handled change is inevitable, so in this

book an attempt has been made to encapsulate a fragment of the mystery before our over-consciousness of the importance of the place, our desire to do the right things by it and our fetish for conservation, takes it all away.

It would be wrong to imagine the fascination of the Gorge is a new phenomenon. The apocalyptic view of industry portrayed by many eighteenth-century writers and artists found its most vivid expression in descriptions and illustrations of Coalbrookdale where the visual contrast between the scenic and picturesque on the one hand and the sublime horrors of the new technology on the other was at its most extreme.

Scene of superfluous grace, and
    wasted bloom,
O, violated COLEBROOK! in an
    hour,
To beauty unpropitious and to song,
Thy Genius of they shades, by
    Plutus brib'd
Amid thy grassy lanes, they
    woodwild glens,
Thy knolls and bubbling wells, they
    rocks, and streams,
Slumbers!—while tribes fuliginous
    invade
The soft, romantic, consecrated
    scenes;
Haunt of the wood-nymph, who
    with airy step,
In times long vanish'd, through thy
    pathless groves
Rang'd;—while the pearly-wristed
    Naiads lean'd,
Braiding their light locks o'er thy
    crystal flood,
Shadowy and smooth . . .
             —Now we view

Their fresh, their fragrant, and their
  silent reign
Usurp't by Cyclops;—hear, in
  mingled tones,
Shout their throng'd barge, their
  pond'rous engines clang
Through thy coy dales; while red
  the countless fires,
With umber'd flames, bicker on thy
  hills,
Dark'ning the Summer's sun with
  columns large
Of thick, sulphureous smoke, which
  spread like palls,
That screen the dead, upon the
  sylvan robe
Of thy aspiring rocks; pollute thy
  gales,
And stain thy glassy waters.—See, in
  troops,
The dusk artificers, with brazen
  throats,
Swarm on thy cliffs, and clamour in
  thy glens,
Steepy and wild, ill suited to such
  guests.

So lamented Anna Seward in the
1780s, but although she clearly
sympathized with the violated wood-
nymphs there is more than a hint of
respect for the dynamic forces of
industry. This ambivalent attitude was
as common amongst those who
commented on the Gorge two hundred
years ago as it is today. In the summer
of 1776, during his tour of Shropshire,
the agricultural journalist Arthur
Young was just as confused.

Colebrook Dale itself is a very
romantic spot, it is a winding glen
between two immense hills which
break into various forms, and all
thickly covered with wood, forming
the most beautiful sheets of hanging
wood. Indeed too beautiful to be

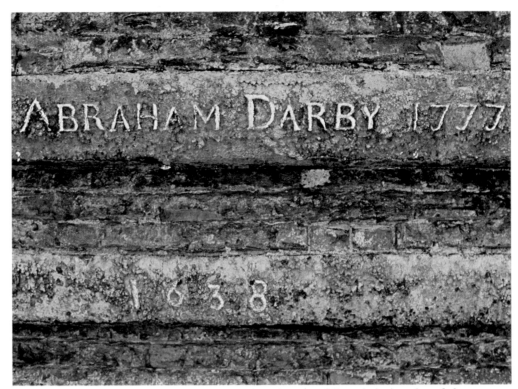

*Beams of the Old Furnace, Coalbrookdale, where iron was first successfully smelted using coke as fuel.*

*Jackfield tileworks at the end of the nineteenth century*

*The Coalbrookdale Company's workmen about 1865*

much in unison with that variety of horrors art has spread at the bottom: the noise of the forges, mills, &c. with all their vast machinery, the flames bursting from the furnaces with the burning of the coal and the smoak of the lime kilns, are altogether sublime, and would unite well with craggy and bare rocks, like St. Vincent's at Bristol.

Accounts of the visual contrasts such as these provide only a partial clue to the significance of the Gorge, but it was not only poets and painters and writers of itineraries who came to see what was going on here. A constant stream of travellers, many from overseas, made their way to the ironworks, mines, canals and railways specifically to learn at first hand of the revolution in technology which was being pioneered here. The period between 1780 and 1820 saw the greatest number. By then the technical pre-eminence of the Gorge was known throughout Europe and North America and Frenchmen, Prussians, Bavarians, Swedes and

Americans all wrote accounts of the district, often in considerable detail. Iron railways were noted at Madeley Wood by French visitors in 1784 whilst in 1819 two Prussian engineers described a dual-gauge plateway in Coalbrookdale of which archaeological evidence has come to light only in recent years. Accurate sketches were made and dimensions recorded so that the most detailed known specification of the inclined plane at Coalport is contained in a drawing published in 1819 by a Frenchman, Jean Dutens. Artists came also, including Thomas Rowlandson, Paul Sandby Munn, John Sell Cotman, Philip James de Loutherbourg and J. M. W. Turner.

The beginnings of significant industrial activity can be traced back to the early seventeenth century when there were numerous small coalmines in the Gorge area, many of them dependent on the navigable River Severn for their access to the outside world. Longwall mining, in contrast to the traditional pillar-and-stall technique, had already

developed in Shropshire by the 1650s whilst wooden railways were in use both above and below ground by about 1610. There were also a few charcoal blast furnaces in which local iron ores were smelted, making the area of considerable industrial importance.

It was one of these furnaces that Abraham Darby took over in 1708. A Quaker, born at Sedgley in 1678, he came to Coalbrookdale from Bristol where he had been involved in the manufacture of brass. In the year following his arrival he perfected a technique for smelting iron ore using coke instead of charcoal as the fuel. Although the implications of this major advance in ironmaking technology were not immediately felt the later large-scale growth of the iron industry on the Shropshire coalfield and ultimately elsewhere in Britian owed much to Darby's innovation.

Much of the demand for iron in the early 1700s was for wrought as opposed to cast iron and coke-smelted pig was unsuitable for this purpose until new refining techniques were developed later in the century. In Coalbrookdale, however, Darby was primarily interested in making castings, notably the iron hollow-ware cooking pots for which he had taken out a patent in 1707. The Coalbrookdale Company developed rapidly on its trade in castings and by mid-century, when coke blast furnaces were being built elsewhere on the Shropshire coalfield, it was beginning to enter its period of greatest importance. Coalbrookdale 'clod' coal from which the coke was made, locally available iron ore, limestone for fluxing and moulding sand, and water to power the blast furnace bellows all contributed to the success of the Company whose products could be sent away by sailing barges on the nearby River Severn.

By 1767 iron rails were being cast at Coalbrookdale, the first in the world, and iron-wheeled vehicles were made to run on them. This was the first stage in the evolution of the metal railway out of the traditional and well-established wooden wagonway and led to the development of the steam railway which revolutionized transport in the nineteenth century. In the late 1770s the Company, by then under the control of Abraham Darby III, grandson of the founder, became deeply involved in another pioneer project: to build an iron bridge across the River Severn about half a mile downstream from Coalbrookdale. Cast in 1779, the erection of the great cast-iron ribs and deck members was supervised by Abraham Darby, and the bridge, the first civil engineering work in the world to utilize iron for its construction, was opened on New Year's Day, 1781. It became an immediate source of wonder, one of the great sights of the age and the central feature of numerous paintings and engravings.

Completion of the bridge, which established a link between Coalbrookdale and the works of John Wilkinson at Willey as well as numerous other works, mines and quarries on the south side of the Severn, led to a reorganization of the road and traffic pattern of the whole neighbourhood and the rapid growth of the small commercial and market town which was to take its name from the bridge. At the time of the bridge's construction the whole section of the

Severn Gorge including the side valley where Darby had established his works was accorded the name Coalbrookdale, but after the development of the town of Ironbridge this name became more restricted in use and eventually only applied to the Dale itself, as it does today.

The latter part of the eighteenth century was the zenith of the Coalbrookdale Company's innovative period. By the time of his death in March 1763 Abraham Darby II had revolutionized the economy of the district with the building of the large new ironworks at Horsehay, carried out with his partner Thomas Goldney, as well as four other major works. After a period of recession during the early 1760s expansion began again under Richard Reynolds, son-in-law of Abraham II, who had control of the

company at this period, and continued with Abraham III. In 1776 the Bedlam or Madeley Wood blast furnaces, built in 1758 on the banks of the Severn, were purchased by Darby, whilst at Donnington Wood, well north of the Gorge, another major ironworks was built with two furnaces erected in 1783 and 1785. Forged iron also became an important aspect of the company's activities and in the early 1780s a water-powered forge was completed at Horsehay, specializing in the manufacture of boiler plates, and a steam-powered forge was opened at Ketley in 1785. In addition, new mining land was leased and limestone quarrying interests were developed so that the Coalbrookdale operation became the largest single iron-making concern in the country and also the focal point of the most celebrated and well-known industrial region.

*Moulding shop in the Upper Works of the Coalbrookdale Company*

In 1789 Abraham Darby III died at the age of thirty-nine, to be buried, like his father, in the little Quaker burial ground overlooking the Upper Furnace Pool. The Company's affairs had become unwieldy and the complex pattern of partnership established between the Darbys and the Reynoldses was causing difficulty. In 1796 the Darby and Reynolds interests were separated, the former retaining the Coalbrookdale and Horsehay works whilst William Reynolds, the son of Richard, took control of the Ketley and Madeley Wood ironworks and associated mines. The turn of the century saw something of a revival in the affairs of the Coalbrookdale Company, with iron bridges and steam engines—many to the designs of James Watt—forming an important part of their output. Richard Trevithick, who through his father had well-established links with Coalbrookdale, was there in 1802 in order to use the Company's expertise in the building of a high-pressure experimental steam engine. Later in the same year he constructed a steam railway locomotive designed to run on the company's plateway and although this was undoubtedly the first railway locomotive to be built anywhere it is not known whether it ran in the Dale.

The architectural use of cast iron was developed in the late 1790s and in the first decade of the nineteenth century the Company was involved in John Nash's alterations to Attingham Hall, supplying the iron frame for the roof of the new picture gallery. This new venture was to have important repercussions, for during the first half of the nineteenth century Coalbrookdale's pre-eminent position in the civil and mechanical engineering

fields was lost to other newer and more adventurous ironworks, notably in the Black Country and South Wales. In two areas however the Company still had an advantage over its competitors; it could produce high quality castings of great complexity—a tribute to its patternmakers and moulders—and at Horsehay it made high quality rolled wrought-iron plate for boilers. There is little doubt that Isambard Kingdom Brunel used Horsehay plate for his mammoth iron ship SS *Great Britain*, launched at Bristol in the 1840s, whilst at a similar period the Coalbrookdale Works was developing a reputation for art castings and architectural ware. The Company's contribution to the Great Exhibition of 1851 was almost entirely in this field and included ornamental gates, a 'boy and swan' fountain and a statue of Andromeda chained to a rock. The gates can still be seen where they were re-erected in Kensington Gardens in 1852, whilst the prototype Andromeda, purchased by Queen Victoria for £300, stands in a pool at Osborne in the Isle of Wight. The boy and swan fountain is beside the preserved Old Furnace at Coalbrookdale. In 1851 the Coalbrookdale works was still the largest single foundry complex in Britain and it remained important throughout most of the nineteenth century. The affairs of the Company as a whole, however, declined considerably and the Darby connection diminished. In the early 1860s the blast furnaces at Horsehay ceased production and the forges were sold in 1886 to become the basis of the present bridge and crane-building concern. The company's furnaces at Lightmoor and Dawley Castle were also blown out, so ending the period of iron smelting. (Iron smelting had ceased in

Coalbrookdale itself in 1818.)

There were many other aspects of industrial activity elsewhere in the Gorge, but the legacy of the Coalbrookdale Company is best seen in the Dale itself where the community of houses and cottages built by or closely associated with the Darbys is still substantially intact. The essential character of a highly developed industrial village still survives as a monument to the social history of the Industrial Revolution period.

On the one hand are the houses built by the Darbys for their own use: The Grange, started by Abraham I but not completed at the time of his death in 1717, the much altered Dale House, now divided into flats with a steel balcony at first floor level, and The Chestnuts where the fourth Abraham Darby was living in 1851. Behind The Chestnuts is the Quaker Burial Ground where all the notable local entrepreneurs, with the exception of Abraham I, are buried. The first Abraham lived at White End near the Upper Forge, which is now demolished, and later at Madeley Court, a fine but decaying mansion which still stands in a semi-derelict state near the village of Madeley. In the 1750s Abraham II built a new house on the top of the hill high above the head of the Dale. This was named Sunniside and was demolished in the mid-nineteenth century. Interspersed amongst these great houses and also on the east side of the Dale are the cottages of the Coalbrookdale Company's employees, many of which still survive, although usually in a poor condition and often unoccupied. Amongst them are some of the first dwellings built specifically for

*A fishing party preparing to leave the Talbot Inn, Ironbridge*

industrial workers, some by the Company itself, others not. The oldest group is Tea Kettle Row, a terrace of six cottages standing behind The Grange and dating from the 1740s, whilst others such as Carpenters' Row, Engine Row and Church Row (formerly Charity Row) came along later in the eighteenth century. Typically these cottages are of one and a half or two storeys and built in rows of six or eight. Frequently rooms of one cottage overlap those of another, whilst at each end of the row is a brewhouse, usually integral with the cottages themselves, where the washing and brewing was done and the pig was hung.

In the centre of the Dale and over-looked by the houses on either side are the remains of the early Coal-brookdale Works established by the Darbys in the eighteenth century, and the present foundry which occupies a larger site further down the valley. At the north end is Upper Furnace Pool, the source of water for the bellows of the Old Furnace, which occupies the confluence of the two streams flowing from the Lightmoor valley to the east and Loamhole Dingle to the north. Below the dam of the pool is the Furnace itself, in substantially the condition Abraham III left it following his modifications of 1777, although now lacking all its ancillary equipment of bellows and waterwheel, casting-shed and pig-bed. Overlooking the site from the south is the Great Warehouse, a four-storey building dating from the 1830s and surmounted by an ornamental cast-iron clock added in 1843.

Lower down Coalbrookdale stand the Wesleyan Chapel, erected in 1885 to commemorate the centenary of the death of the evangelical John Fletcher of Madeley, Holy Trinity Church of 1854, and the Coalbrookdale Literary and Scientific Institute built by the company in 1859. Further south towards the River Severn is the now overgrown site of Lower Forge Pool with nearby Rose Cottages and the site of the boring mill set up in the late eighteenth century for finishing the cylinders of steam engines. The wide grass verge along the side of the road here was occupied until the late nineteenth century by an iron plateway which ran from the works to a wharf on the River Severn. This wharf has recently been uncovered and the adjacent warehouse, built in the 1840s in the Gothic manner, is currently under restoration. It is here, at Dale End, that Coalbrookdale merges into Ironbridge.

Now Coalbrookdale, like the rest of the Ironbridge Gorge, rests in a limbo between past and future. Still retaining its essential character and the all-pervading atmosphere of its auspicious beginnings, it is recognized and respected, but is infinitely too subtle to be grasped. Under pressure from traffic and visitors and, worse still, from uncontrollable desires to enhance the place, Coalbrookdale hovers in a no-man's-land. The blue smoke from the modern cupola furnaces of the works still hangs below the trees of the valley sides, but now it is at one with the wood-nymphs and naiads.

Although Coalbrookdale provided the

15

initial focal point for the industrial growth of the Gorge the sides of the Severn valley itself for some two miles downstream from Dale End became thronged with industrial and commercial activity during the nineteenth century. Even before the construction of the Iron Bridge and the growth of the town around it river traffic was considerable, particularly from the eastern or Coalbrookdale end of the Gorge. Writing in the *Gentleman's Magazine* in 1758 George Perry claimed that 'upwards of 100,000 tons of coals are annually shipped from collieries about Broseley and Madeley to the towns situate on its banks, and from thence into the adjacent counties; also great quantities of grain, pig and bar iron, iron manufactures and earthenwares; as well as wool, hops, cyder and provisions, are constantly exported to Bristol and other places from whence merchants' goods are brought in return. The freight from Shrewsbury to Bristol is about 10s. per ton, and from Bristol to Shrewsbury about 15s., the rates to the intermediate towns being in proportion.'

He noted two sorts of vessel in use on the river, a small type between 40 and 60 feet long with a single mast and a carrying capacity of 20 to 40 tons, which he called a barge or frigate, and a much larger trow of 40 to 80 tons with a mast up to 80 feet high and square sails. Some had mizen masts; they were generally 16 to 20 feet wide, 60 feet long and when new and completely rigged cost about £300. Perry commissioned an exact list of the barges and trows on the River Severn which in 1756 totalled 376 in use between Welshpool and Gloucester. Of these no fewer than 139 were owned in the Gorge.

Downstream from Ironbridge the Bedlam blast furnaces at Madeley Wood were in operation down to the 1830s and there were similar concentrations of iron-making activity on the other side of the river at the Calcutts. The opening of another new bridge at about the same time as the Iron Bridge at the downstream end of the Gorge near Preens Eddy stimulated further commercial growth here and by the early years of the nineteenth century, largely as a result of the energies of William Reynolds, a miniature new town had been built which became known as Coalport. Here in 1787 Reynolds began driving an adit into the hillside a few feet above river flood level and about half a mile upstream from the Preens Eddy bridge. He discovered a spring of natural bitumen which was commercially exploited. In 1799 it was described as yielding only some thirty gallons a week, but at first this had been nearly a thousand gallons. Known as the Tar Tunnel, this thousand-yard passage into the hillside has been partially cleared of debris and is now accessible to the public.

The real growth of this area however came with the building of the Shropshire Canal running from Donnington Wood in the north of the coalfield through Oakengates and Madeley to the River Severn. The descent from the high ground of the coalfield to the riverside was by means of a remarkable inclined plane. Boats were lowered into a basin beside the river and then ran parallel to the Severn for half a mile to a terminal basin upstream of the bridge. This canal/river interchange became the focal point of Reynolds's new community of Coalport, which gave its name to the china works and also the bridge. Reynolds was not only responsible for the roads, housing and ferry, but actively encouraged new industries such as chain-making and the highly successful Coalport porcelain factory.

During the nineteenth century the nature of the economy in the Gorge changed gradually as after 1850 tile-making developed on the Jackfield side of the river and the Bedlam blast furnaces closed to be replaced by a much bigger iron smelting complex beside the canal at Blists Hill. The tileworks assumed very considerable importance towards the end of the century and one of them, Maw's, had become the largest in the world by the 1880s. During the same period Iron-bridge became a thriving shopping and commercial centre despite the fall-off in river traffic after the opening of the Severn Valley Railway in 1862. Numerous fashionable houses were built on the upper, south-facing slopes of the Gorge above the bridge and the place settled into a prosperous and stable community which survived intact down to and even after the First World War.

The nature of decline in the Gorge is difficult to analyse as it was a slow and insidious process spread over many years. As the economy gradually ran down, a creeping neglect and dereliction set in; young people left the area and houses and cottages became empty. The Coalport end of the Shropshire Canal closed as early as the 1890s, to be followed by Blists Hill blast furnaces in 1912 and the migration in 1926 of the Coalport china company from their riverside works to Stoke-on-Trent.

*Coalbrookdale in the 1880s with the Works on the left and the Institute in the right foreground*

*The* William *of Broseley, owner Thomas Beard, one of the last sailing barges in the Gorge, about 1900. In the background is Maw's tileries*

In Coalbrookdale the ironworks continued, to be taken over by Allied Ironfounders in the 1920s, who were in turn absorbed into Glynwed in 1969. At Dale End however the short-lived foundry closed and the buildings eventually became the Merrythought teddy-bear factory. The river traffic ceased altogether in the early 1900s and the wharves and warehouses fell into disuse. Thus the neo-gothic warehouse of the Coalbrookdale Company became a mineral water bottling factory and later still a garage.

After the Second World War the decline accelerated following the closure first of the Craven Dunnill tile works and then of Maw's, and also the two railways in the Gorge. By then however the problems of decline in the whole East Shropshire coalfield area had become a cause of great concern resulting in the designation of part of the area, including the Gorge, as Dawley New Town. This was later expanded to embrace the whole coalfield, including Wellington and Oakengates, and was called Telford in honour of the civil engineer who started his career in Shropshire. As Telford New Town developed, however, the initial effect on the Gorge was to accentuate the problems of neglect and dereliction. Housing estates with their own shopping precincts were built along the northern edge of the river valley and this, together with the growth of the main town centre shopping area, drained away trade still further.

But the arrival of the new town coincided with an awakening of interest in the area. As early as 1959 Allied Ironfounders had opened to the public the Darby furnace site, carefully

17

*The tollhouse at Coalport in the late nineteenth century*

*The characters from Jackfield carnival outside the Robin Hood Inn about 1905*

excavated and restored, together with a small museum of ironfounding, to commemorate the 250th anniversary of the coke smelting process. This and the rising national interest in the remains of the Industrial Revolution began to focus people's attention on the Gorge and its remarkable range of industrial artefacts.

The growth of industrial archaeology as a popular study was merely one facet of the new interest in the environment and its conservation which had its origins in the post-war years and reached its culmination in the high-rise sixties. The conservation movement itself produced new legislation, some of which stemmed from the rather doubtful ethics of the civic trust syndrome which had gripped the articulate middle classes, and as a result Coalbrookdale and parts of Ironbridge became a Conservation Area. Later the small number of listed buildings in this area was greatly expanded, to over 250, partly as an emergency action to prevent demolitions but also in an attempt to stem a rising tide of 'unacceptable' alterations.

In the meantime further awareness of the historical and archaeological attributes of the Gorge had resulted in the setting up in 1968 of the Ironbridge Gorge Museum Trust with the active encouragement of Telford Development Corporation. This new organization had as its objectives the preservation for all time of the important industrial sites of the Gorge area and the creation of an open-air museum on a derelict 42-acre site at Blists Hill where industrial processes important in East Shropshire could be re-created in an appropriate setting. In

1970 the Trust took over on a long-term lease the Abraham Darby furnace site and associated museum and, since then, on funds raised largely by appeals to industry, it has been instrumental in the restoration of a number of sites including the Iron Bridge itself. Rose Cottages and Carpenters' Row in Coalbrookdale are being restored by the Trust and the Severn Wharf and Warehouse beside the river are being adapted to form the basis for a visitor centre. Bedlam furnaces have been partially excavated, the section of the Shropshire Canal at Blists Hill has been cleared and re-watered, and track is in place again on the great inclined plane at Coalport. The motives for all this activity are primarily archaeological and historical in that the Trust is anxious to ensure not only the survival of important sites, but proper standards of excavation and research, restoration and interpretation.

This work solves only part of the problem of the Gorge, and in turn it creates others. Large numbers of people coming into the area bring access and traffic difficulties, and whilst their spending power can marginally assist a flagging economy the straightforward commercial response in most places to numerous visitors is almost inevitably tawdry and environmentally damaging. In an area such as the Ironbridge Gorge these types of response could have disastrous consequences. The problems of the Gorge are further complicated by the absence of main drainage, several areas of unstable ground and increasing pressure of through traffic. In these cases however the problem and the solution are at least definable. A

sewerage programme is now in hand, areas of instability have been identified and can be avoided in any future schemes of development and, although some of the through traffic routes are complex and difficult to readjust, the major pressures can possibly be solved by a new link road from the head of the Dale to Buildwas, by peripheral car parks and a park-and-ride system and manipulation of the pattern of roads and river crossings in the Gorge proper. The capital costs of this work are enormous and exceed anything that would be required for specific conservation work in the Gorge itself. This is only right because what the place needs most is protection from the outside world.

But the historical and visual aspects of the Gorge and its landscape are much more difficult to deal with and so far they have eluded everybody. The superficiality of existing conservation legislation which dwells unduly on the more obvious common denominators of visual amenity offers little help as the Gorge lies outside accepted contemporary standards of aesthetic appreciation. There is little consciously conceived architecture in the Gorge, but there are many buildings of which each one reflects the simple aspirations of its builders—to stand up, to fulfil its function, perhaps to face the sunshine or command a view and only on odd occasions to make a gesture to the outside world as an expression of status. Similarly the wilderness of vegetation which envelops much of the valley is there because of history, an essential element of the overall landscape but in no way quantifiable. The crude laws of conservation, of neatness and tidiness, of colour-wash and tasteful street furniture, of British

Standard birch trees in nicely detailed brick paving and log-edged car parks are all defied by a place which is so totally a function of its past, and its past is exceptional.

The Severn Gorge is a place of elusive quality derived largely from its history. Any ill-considered or careless action by individuals or by the authorities could easily damage, perhaps irrevocably, the essential character of the area. Even the sense of decay, and the feeling that time has stood still, are ingredients which impart a particular quality to places like Ironbridge, Coalbrookdale and Jackfield.

The keynote of any policy plan must therefore be the need for great care and thought in the preparation and implementation of any proposals. It is appropriate to talk of the area in terms of a trust. The voices of the past demand that we do nothing to damage the heritage which by great good fortune has been handed down to us. Equally, the voices of the future require that we pass on these valuable assets to future generations in such a way that they too can appreciate the qualities which are evident to us today.

The Severn Gorge is special. It is because it is special that individuals and authorities alike will have to accept restraints on the actions which can be taken. It is because it is special that we must seek to justify the considerable sums of money that will have to be spent if we are to rescue the area from the fifty years of decline which have produced the present problems.

*

Here is enlightenment of a high order
from Telford Development Corporation's press release announcing
proposals for the preservation of the
'birthplace of the Industrial
Revolution'. But heady stuff such as
this requires much more than a policy
plan and a project group to ensure that
the totality of the landscape actually
*does* survive substantially intact.

It requires a ready awareness that
ideas and attitudes evolve as the result
of thinking and talking and that the
spending of time to consult, to learn
and to research cannot be bypassed if
the policy statement is to be met in the
spirit as well as in the letter.
Nevertheless, the future of the Gorge
must be seen in the context of the new
town of Telford, and Telford has a
responsibility to the world to seek out
the right sort of answers.

To some extent the problem, as with
all major areas of conservation
concern, lies not only with the
individuals who wish to alter their
properties, fell their trees or render
their brickwork, however 'insensitive'
their actions may be, but with the very
statutory bodies in whose hands on a
macro-scale the future of the landscape
lies. The reconciliation of the voices of
past and future with the obvious
necessities of everyday life today
demands much more than considerable
sums of money which in themselves can
be a recipe for disaster. It requires
understanding in depth as well as
breadth, a detailed archaeological,
historical and ecological appreciation
of *why* what is there *is* there, a
conscious ability to exercise restraint
and a dedication to do nothing when
nothing might be the right answer, but
above all a sense of humility.

*The photographs on pages 11–18 are
reproduced by courtesy of the Ironbridge
Gorge Museum Trust.*

The area of Abraham Darby's furnace was cleared of debris in the late 1950s by the then owners, Allied Ironfounders, and, together with a museum of ironfounding, it became one of the first industrial sites to be made accessible to the public on a regular basis. Now administered by the Ironbridge Gorge Museum Trust, the museum and furnace site are open every day of the year. The Old Furnace (*facing page*) and later Snapper Furnace (*right*), a Coalbrookdale-built locomotive (*below right*) and cast-iron wheels running on cast-iron rails are amongst the outdoor features of the site.

The Great Warehouse, built by the Coalbrookdale Company in the 1830s, now marks the division between the active foundry to the south and the Abraham Darby furnace site farther up the Dale. Iron is used extensively in its construction with cast window lintels, frames and sills and cast-iron columns supporting the floors. Nevertheless the floors and floor beams themselves are timber and the clock, added in 1843 and built largely of iron, is supported on a massive timber frame.

'Most housewives did their own
laundry-work and baking and some
brewed their own beer. The barm
for baking could be obtained on
certain days at any of the inns, and
small beer could be had for 3d a
bucketful, which made a good
dinner beverage. The washing had
to be taken to the mangle room,
which was a noted gossiping-place.
Water for domestic use had to be
carried to most of the houses in the
Upper Dale, from Bathwell pump
or from the pump which used to be
in the foundry. This was the only
supply of clean water, except for a
few lucky ones who had wells.
Many women carried their own
water from the pumps, and it was
not unusual to see a woman
carrying a pail of water on her
head, supported by a round cloth
pad. Coal was fetched from the
coal-pen in half-hundredweights or
hundredweights, which cost 4d per
hundredweight for coal and 2d per
hundredweight for slack.'
Charles F. Peskin, *Memories of Old
Coalbrookdale*, 1941

'Coalbrook Dale, a winding glen two miles from Madeley, hemmed in by lofty hills and hanging woods, is celebrated for the most considerable iron works in England: the forges, mills, and steam engines, with all their vast machinery—the flaming furnaces, and smoking chimneys, the handsome residences nestling under the cliffs of the hills, have altogether a most romantic and singular appearance, and perhaps in no part of the globe are features of so diversified and wonderful a character brought together within so limited a compass—here art has triumphed over nature, and the barren wilderness has been converted into one of the most animating abodes of commerce, and being studded with residences of taste and elegance, it gives the whole a very interesting appearance.'
Samuel Bagshaw, *History, Gazetteer, and Directory of Shropshire*, 1851

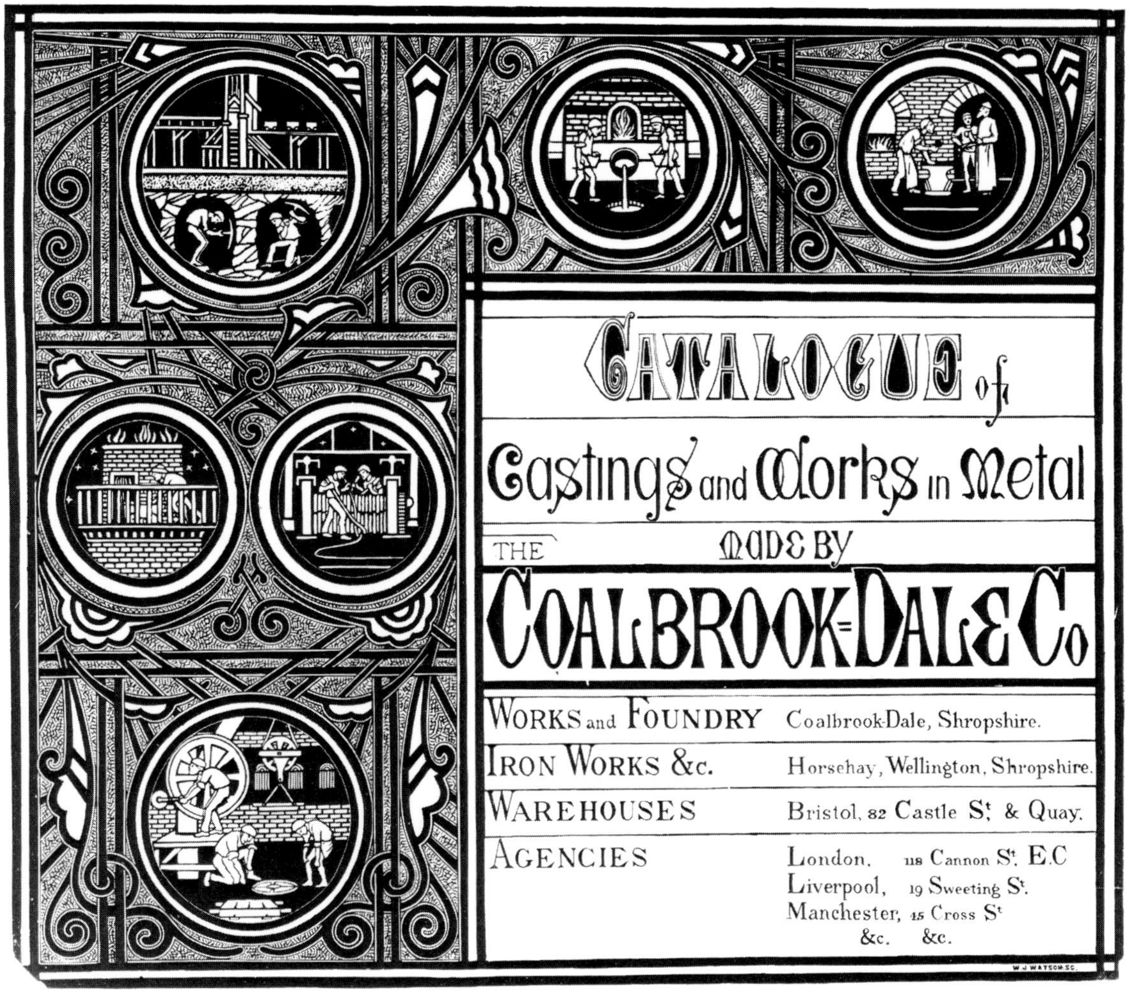
CATALOGUE of
Castings and Works in Metal
THE MADE BY
COALBROOK-DALE Co
WORKS and FOUNDRY Coalbrook-Dale, Shropshire.
IRON WORKS &c. Horsehay, Wellington, Shropshire.
WAREHOUSES Bristol, 82 Castle St. & Quay.
AGENCIES London, 118 Cannon St. E.C
Liverpool, 19 Sweeting St.
Manchester, 45 Cross St
&c. &c.

The catalogues of the Coalbrookdale Company from the 1860s onwards demonstrate the brilliantly successful metamorphosis through which the works went during the middle years of the nineteenth century when, as bigger, more modern and more efficient ironworks elsewhere in Britain took away much of the heavy civil and mechanical engineering casting work on which the Company had depended, it was able to enter the new field of decorative and architectural cast-iron ware, based on the skill of its pattern-makers and mould-makers.

Stove grates (valve backs and bivalve backs), stove grates (medieval), dog grates, chimney pieces, fenders (scroll, circular, gothic and elliptic), fenders (heavy for large openings), hall tables, hat and coat stands, umbrella stands, shoe scrapers, door porters, garden chairs, fountains (garden) and fountains (ornamental), iron vases and pedestals, flower stands and garden rollers were just a small selection from one of the many catalogues of the mid-1870s.

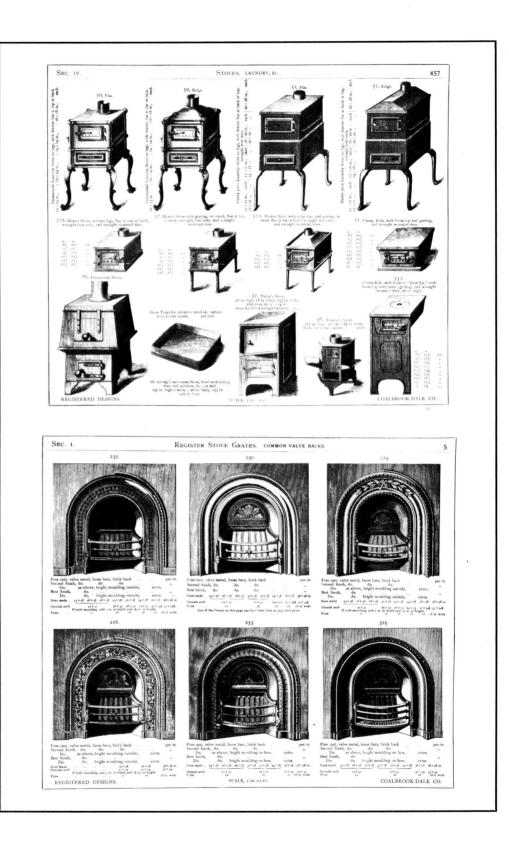

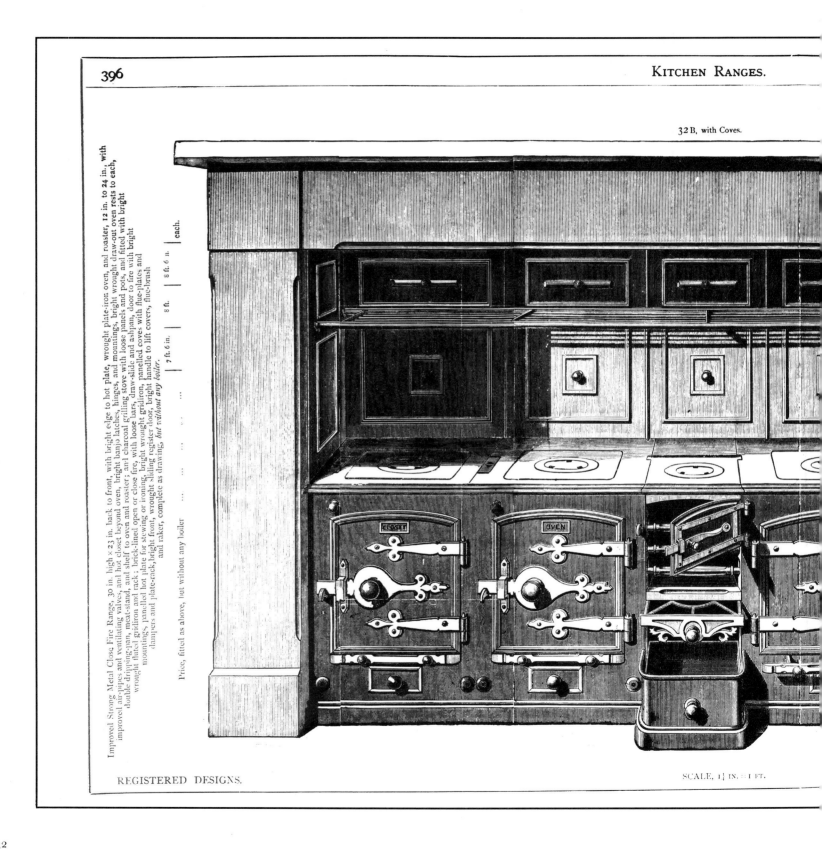

32 B, with Coves.

Improved Strong Metal Close Fire Range, 30 in. high × 23 in. back to front, with bright edge to hot plate, wrought plate-iron oven, and roaster, 12 in. to 24 in., with improved air-pipes and ventilating valves, and hot closet beyond oven, bright banjo latches, hinges, and mountings, bright wrought draw-out oven rests to each, double dripping-pan, meat-stand, and shelf to oven and roaster; and charcoal grilling stove with loose panels and pots, and fitted with bright wrought thatoll gridiron and rack : brick-lined open or close fire, with loose bars, draw-slide and ashpan, door to fire with bright mountings, panelled hot plate for stewing or ironing, bright wrought gridiron, panelled coves with flue-plates and dampers and plate-rack, bright front, wrought sliding register door, bright handle to lift covers, flue-brush and raker, complete as drawing, *but without any boiler.*

| | 7 ft. 6 in. | 8 ft. | 8 ft. 6 in. | each. |

Price, fitted as above, but without any boiler    ...    ...    ...    ...

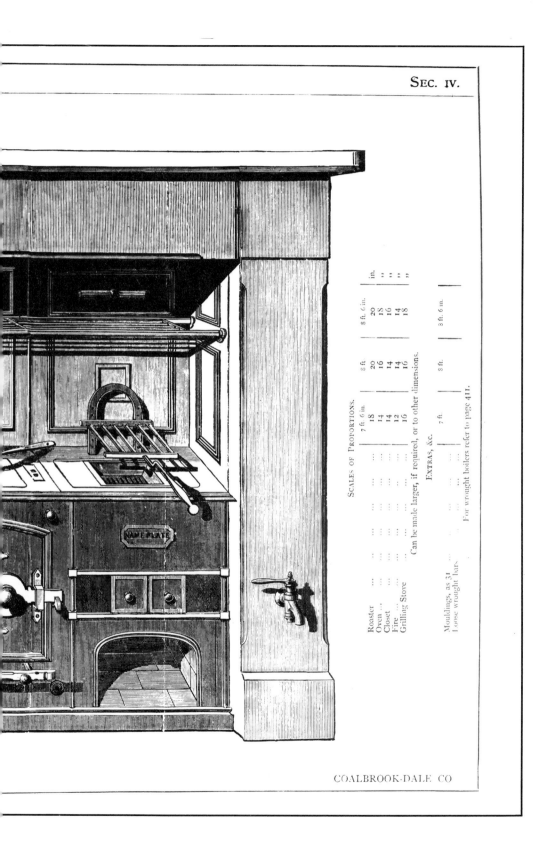

### SCALES OF PROPORTIONS.

| | 7 ft. 6 in. | 8 ft. | 8 ft. 6 in. | in. |
|---|---|---|---|---|
| Roaster | 18 | 20 | 20 | |
| Oven | 14 | 16 | 18 | |
| Closet | 14 | 14 | 16 | |
| Fire | 12 | 14 | 14 | |
| Grilling Stove | 16 | 16 | 18 | |

Can be made larger, if required, or to other dimensions.

### EXTRAS, &c.

| | 7 ft. | 8 ft. | 8 ft. 6 in. |
|---|---|---|---|
| Mouldings, as 31 | | | |
| Loose wrought bars | | | |

For wrought boilers refer to page 411.

COALBROOK-DALE CO

Kitchen ranges became a Coalbrookdale speciality and this model of about 1875, Number 32B with coves, was one of the largest. The Company's catalogues and promotional literature relied heavily on fine and detailed engravings, precise dimensions and a subtle and dignified restraint in advertising terminology: *improved* air pipes; *best* boiler plate; *bright* handle to lift covers; *good* brass cock; *strong* plate-iron roaster; *ground* nameplate; *patent* damper.

The railway did not come through Coalbrookdale until 1864, when the Great Western Railway line from Wellington and Shifnal to Buildwas Junction on the Severn Valley line was opened. Although closed to passengers in 1962 it still carries coal and oil trains for the Ironbridge power stations.

The line skirts the Darby furnace site on a brick viaduct which forms a major visual element in this section of the Dale. Some of the arches contain discarded moulding boxes (*left*) from the foundry; others house the earth closets of the cottages across the road.

Tea Kettle Row, dating from the 1740s, is the oldest surviving group of workers' cottages in Coalbrookdale and, although not built by the Company itself, it represents a prototype for numerous subsequent rows of company-built housing of which a few examples still remain.

Later cottages were built piecemeal throughout the eighteenth and much of the nineteenth centuries with little evolution in general design or layout. Cast-iron chimney pots were used extensively.

'The Face of the Country shews the happy Effects of this flourishing Trade, the lower class of People, who are very numerous here, are enabled to live comfortably; their Cottages, which almost cover some of the neighbouring Hills, are throng'd with healthy Children, who soon are able to find Employment and perhaps cheerfulness and contentment are not more visible in any other place.' George Perry, *A Description of Coalbrookdale* . . ., 1758

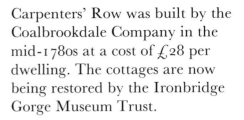

Carpenters' Row was built by the Coalbrookdale Company in the mid-1780s at a cost of £28 per dwelling. The cottages are now being restored by the Ironbridge Gorge Museum Trust.

From the 1850s until well into this century cast-iron was used to mark the graves of those buried in the churchyard of Holy Trinity, Coalbrookdale. Dark, purple-brown rust protects the inscriptions in perpetuity, a patina as permanent, subtle and expressive in its own way of the nature of the material which supports it as anything acquired by bronze.

A prominent feature of the Coalbrookdale landscape is the Institute, built by the Company from their own blue bricks, and completed in 1859. The Coalbrookdale Literary & Scientific Institution was formed in 1853 and was followed three years later by a School of Art, set up with the object of promoting better standards of design for art castings made in the ironworks. The new building, built to the design of the works manager, Mr Charles Crookes, and in a style described at the time as 'Tudor Gothic', provided a home for both bodies, with a lecture hall, reading room, art room, library and attached house for the librarian. The roof of the main building was altered to the present mansard style in the 1930s in order to increase the accommodation. Today the Institute is empty.

In the early 1920s the Coalbrookdale war memorial was inserted into a bay in the cast-iron railings. It too was cast, although in bronze rather than iron.

The Grange, known also as Rosehill and the Great House, is the central feature of the little nucleus of buildings in Coal-brookdale overlooking Upper Furnace Pool and the blast furnace site. Here many of the Darbys lived in houses interspersed with the cottages of their work-people close to the source of their prosperity and close also to the needs of the community in whose welfare and well-being they were deeply interested and involved.

The Grange is probably the house started by Abraham Darby I but not completed at the time of his death in 1717. Together with the adjacent coach house (*far right*), it has been acquired by the Ironbridge Gorge Museum Trust.

The initials of Francis Darby and the date 1839 mark the iron gates beside the entrance to the Quaker Burial Ground in Coalbrookdale.

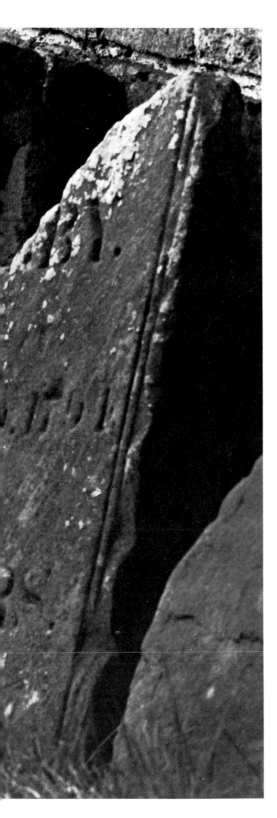

Two giant Wellingtonias supervise the secret enclosure of the Quaker Burial Ground, high on the upper slopes of Coalbrookdale. Here, within the wall built to keep out deer from the adjacent park, lie all the notable Darbys, with the exception of Abraham I who is buried in Broseley. Most significant are the second Abraham, who in the 1750s built the Horsehay ironworks, his son Abraham III, builder of the Iron Bridge, and William Reynolds, a grandson of Abraham II and himself one of the most successful of the great Shropshire ironmasters. The stones in the burial ground have been removed from their original positions to line the surrounding wall.

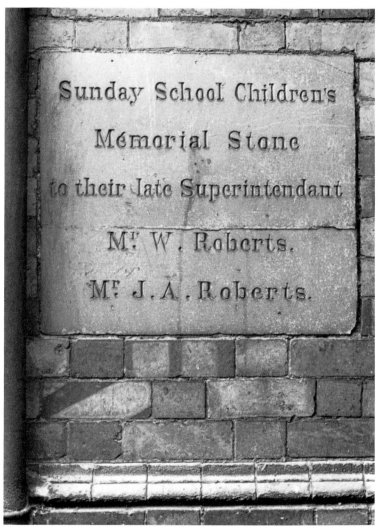

Sunday School Children's
Memorial Stone
to their late Superintendant
M.ʳ W. Roberts.
M.ʳ J.A. Roberts.

Erected in 1885 to commemorate the centenary of the death of the evangelist vicar of Madeley, John Fletcher, the Wesleyan Chapel in Coalbrookdale now stands empty and gutted of furniture and fittings.

The only industrial significance of the River Severn today in the vicinity of the Gorge is as a source of cooling water for Ironbridge power stations. Standing on flat ground at the entrance to the Gorge itself the 'A' station was built in the 1930s, to be followed nearly forty years later by the massive 'B' station with its four great cooling towers. Specially tinted to make them more compatible with the surrounding earth-colour, they crowd and jostle into the view upstream from Ironbridge and Dale End, magnificent, cyclopean, organic and alive.

Loadcroft Wharf on the Severn at
Dale End was the point from which
the Coalbrookdale Company's iron
goods were shipped away down
river to Stourport, Bristol and the
rest of the world. Linked to the
works by an iron tramway, the
wharf was one of the major sources
of river traffic, and in the 1840s the
Company built itself a brick
warehouse here in the Gothic
manner in order to store goods
prior to shipment. The bizarre
architectural style of this humorous
building is further heightened by
the gentle Piranesian decay of the
polychrome brickwork in pink and
yellow, trimmed with rock plants
and a small ash tree in the chimney.
The half-hexagonal lady chapel
housed the tally clerks and gave
them a view out over the wharf
itself.

Gas conduit handrails, primeval light fittings and brick gullies are perhaps more susceptible than many other details of the Gorge landscape to the attentions of the tidy conservationist hooked on the myth of 'enhancement'.

The Wharfage, running alongside the river from the Severn Wharf and Warehouse towards Tontine Hill and the Iron Bridge, still expresses perfectly the commercial and residential ambivalence of Ironbridge with its mixture of warehouses, pubs, houses and odd inserted shops. It is a critical area for the future of the town, the most run-down and the most challenging. It could degenerate into a riverside walk in response to the visitor amenity syndrome, but do visitors really want to come to a place visually engineered for their benefit? The intrinsic qualities of the Wharfage, of good straight-forward buildings eminently suitable for a continued existence as houses, shops or offices, if carefully treated need no doctoring and, above all, should not be diminished by unsympathic new uses which might take away their relevance to the past and to the very name—Wharfage. The character of Ironbridge comes through very clearly from the entries in the Commercial Directory.

# Commercial Directory

Agar John, greengrocer and butcher, High street

Alcock Bertha, confectioner, Wharfage

Asbury Wm., innkeeper and brewer, Old House inn, Madeley Wood green

Aston The Misses E. and M. A., milliners, Market sq

Bailey Beriah, lic. vict. and brewer, Three Tuns hotel, High st

Barber Wm., shoemaker, Madeley rd

Bartlam Charles Ruby, ironmonger, tinsmith, lamp and oil merchant, Tontine bank

Bates Edwin, tailor and draper, Madeley hill

Baugh Jane, hairdresser and fancy

goods dealer, Tontine hill

Beddoes Frank Green, ironmonger, tinsmith and bellhanger, High st

Blockley James, joiner, Hodge bower

Board School, Hill side; David Thomas, master; Miss Clark, infants

Booth Thomas, tile layer, Church ter

Branford John, painter, plumber and decorator, Madeley rd

Briscoe John, farmer, Hill farm

British Workman Coffee House Company—Isaac Taylor, manager; J. Slater, sec.—Wharfage

Broadfield Richard, labourer, Madeley rd

**BUCK CHRISTIAN, lic. vict. and mineral water manufacturer, wine and spirit merchant, &c., White Hart, Wharfage**

Burd George, solicitor and clerk to the magistrates, commissioner for oaths, perpetual commission agent for the Royal Insurance Company, Waterloo st

**COLDICOTT CHAS. WM., agent for the Scottish Widows', Railway Passengers' Accident, and the Imperial Accidental Insurance Companies, Station House, Railway Station**

Cheshire David H., moulder, Lincoln hill

Chubb Montague, clerk, Lincoln view

Clegg Susannah Mary, tobacconist, Wharfage

Cookson James, fancy goods dealer, High st

—— Wm., grocer and general dealer, Hodge bower

Corfield Alfred, grocer and provision dealer, Waterloo

**CORLETT THOMAS, watchmaker, jeweller and optician, High st**

**CURZON GEORGE & SON, painters and plumbers, Madeley wood**

**CURZON GEORGE, innkeeper and brewer, Fox inn, Madeley wood**

Darrall Ephraim, glass and china dealers, High st

Davies Ed. Oliver, ironmonger's assistant, Severn ter

Dickin Francis, grocer and Italian warehouseman, Tontine hill

"Dicks" boot and shoe warehouse—Martin Dufficy, local manager—High st

Dixon and Lane, provision merchants, Waterloo st

—— Alfred, boot, shoe and general dealer, High st

——Alfred, draper, ironmonger, milliner and general dealer, High st

—— Thomas, moulder, Lincoln hill

Dodd Wm., foreman brickmaker, Madeley hill

Drennan John, supervisor of Inland Revenue, Primrose cottage

Dunbar John, grocer and agent for the Prudential Assurance Co., Madeley rd

Eaton Thomas, clothier and outfitter, High street

Edge Frederick Wm., compositor, Church terrace

Edwards Arthur, shoeing and general smith, Madeley rd

—— Jane, licensed victualler, White Horse, Lincoln house

—— Rev. Lloyd, rector of Jackfield

—— Edward Thomas, watchman, Lincoln hill

Evans Henry, joiner, Woodlands

—— Thomas, draper and tea dealer, Hill Top house

—— Wm., mason, Lincoln hill

Ferrington Eliza, general draper, High st

Fowler Nathaniel, innkeeper, Horse and Jockey, Madeley wood

Franks Brothers, grocers, bakers and provision merchants, Madeley rd

—— Wm., Waterloo st

French John, Inland Revenue officer, Rose villa

Gadsby Wm., Hill side

Garrard George Mingay, superintendent of tileries, Charnock house

Gauton Jane, marine store, Church hill

Gottheimer Aaron, tobacconist, High st

Grainger Francis Hughes, licensed vict. and brewer, George and Dragon, Madeley rd

Grant Alexander, general draper and milliner, High st

**GROVES EDWIN FLETCHER, wine and spirit merchant and brewer, Severn brewery, High st, agent for D'Arcy's Dublin stout and for Allsopp's Burton ales, ale and porter merchant, bottler, &c.**

Hancock John, smith, Hodge bower

Harris Edward, grocer, &c., Madeley rd

—— James, grocer, Madeley rd

**HARWOOD CHARLES PHILLIPS, fishing tackle manufacturer, Tontine hill**

Hayward George, miner, Madeley wood

Hill Henry, grocer and baker, High st

Hinsley Eleanor G., milliner and fancy draper, Market sq

Holder Charles, fitter, Hodge bower

Hughes Wm., moulder, Madeley rd

Ironbridge Gaslight Company—Joseph Hy. Jones, manager; Frederick Chubb, secretary

——Coalbrookdale and Shropshire Permanent Benefit Building Society—David White, sec.

—— and Coalbrookdale Co-operative Society—Arthur B. Green, manager —Wharfage

James Elizabeth, general dealer, Tontine hill

Jinks John, chemist, Bridge end

Johnson John, ladies' school, Brock Holes house

Jones Eliza, cabinetmaker and upholsterer, and furniture dealer, Madeley rd

—— Joseph Hy., manager of Ironbridge Gaslight Company, Gas house

—— Richard, innkeeper, malster and brewer, Wheat Sheaf, Wharf st

Jordan Theophilus Edmund, confectioner and fishing tackle manufacturer, High st

Ketley Mary Ann, licensed victualler and brewer, Royal Oak, Church hill

Langford Robert, hairdresser, tobacconist and emigration agent, High st

Langston Jacob, lic. vict. and brewer, Block house, Madeley wood

Legge George and Son, manufacturers of bricks and tiles, The Woodlands, Madeley

Lindop Wm., moulder, Hodge bower

Lloyd Thomas Wm., lic. vict. and brewer, Queen's Head hotel, High st

Lucas Ann, milliner and fancy draper, High st

Madeley Wood Company, brick and tile manufacturers, white brick works, Madeley wood—Wm. Simpson, manager

Marshall Wm., station master, Coalbrookdale station, Wharfage

Lloyds, Barnetts and Bosanquet's Bank, Limited—Thomas Powell, manager

Lloyd Wm. and Sons, painters, paperhangers and builders, Madeley rd

Nevett Ann Amelia, printer, stationer and fancy repository, Tontine hill

—— Robert, organist of St. Luke's, Ivy Cottage, Church hill

**NEVETT ROBERT, surveyor, builder, contractor and monumental mason, agent for the Salop Fire, Guardian Fire and Life and the Rock Freehold Land Society, Ivy cottage, Church hill**

Norton Edwin, fishmonger and fruiterer, Wharfage

Norry Eliza, New cottage

Oliver Joseph, gardener, New cottage

Osborne Joseph, watchmaker, High st

Owen Edward, maltster, The Grove

—— Edward, rope maker, River view

—— George, innkeeper and brewer, Railway tavern, High st

—— Jas., grocer and provision merchant, High st

—— Harry, maltster, Wharfage

Oliver Wm., grocer and butcher, Madeley wood

Onions Wm., coal dealer, Wharfage

Parrock Jane, lic. vict. and brewer, Crown inn, Waterloo st

Parton Thomas, draper, hatter and undertaker, Market sq

**PATTON THOMAS EDWIN, rate and tax collector, accountant and collector to the Madeley Local Board, collector of income tax,**

and house & estate agent, Providence place, Church hill

**PATTON THOMAS EDWIN,** agent for the Life Association of Scotland, London and Lancashire Fire, the Northern Accidental Insurance Company, the Rock Freehold Land Society, agent and collector of tithes for the Vicar of Madeley, and estate agent to J. E. Bartlett, Poverill court, Aylesbury

**PELLOWE HY.,** stationer, printer and news-agent, Tontine bank

**PELLOWE HENRY,** local representative of the "Shropshire Evening News," "Eddowes' Journal," and the "Wellington Journal," Tontine bank

**PERKS EDWARD,** family butcher, Tontine hill

Perks Misses Susan and Elizabeth, dressmakers, Wharfage

—— Wm. Paddock, refreshment rooms, confectioner and beer retailer, High st

Phillips Wm., pork butcher and cattle dealer, Waterloo st

Poole Ann, innkeeper and brewer, Bird-in-Hand, Madeley wood

—— George, grocer and newsagent, Madeley rd

Potts Andrew, butcher, High st

Powell Thomas, agent for the National Provident Institution, Lloyd's bank

Preston Alfred, railway porter, Madeley rd

Price Thomas, builder, Brock holes

Prince Vincent, clerk, Madeley rd

Procter James, surgeon, medical officer to Madeley Union, Ironbridge Dispensary, and Coalbrookdale Ironworks, Severn villa

Redmond Sergeant, drill instructor, Hodge bower

Reeves John, painter, Madeley rd

Rickers Thomas, miner, Wharfage

Roberts Edwin, brewer and licensed vict., Robin Hood, Madeley wood

—— John, grocer's assistant, Lincoln hill

—— Richard, timber merchant's manager, Ward's row

—— Sarah, agent for Gilbey and Co's wines and spirits and Allsopps' ales, Primrose cottage

Rowley Thomas, painter, Hodge bower

Rutter John, fitter, Lincoln hill

Scott Mrs. B. H., baker and confectioner, High st

Shepstone Caroline, umbrella maker and dealer, High st

Shingler Jane, hatter, bootmaker and outfitter, High st

Shorthouse Wm. Henry, head master, Wesleyan schools, Madeley rd

Slater Joseph, agent for the Manchester Fire and Star Life Insurance offices, Market sq

—— Joseph, Sarah and Annie, printers stationers, bookbinders, booksellers

and newsagents, Market square

Smith Egerton W., wholesale and retail grocer and provision merchant, High st

Smith Wm., dairyman, Bath place

—— Wm. Henry, registrar of births, deaths and marriages, Belle vue

Stanway Fanny, dressmaker, Severn bank

Stevens Joseph, marine store, Hill side

Stodd John, bootmaker, Tontine hill

—— William, outfitter, clothier and bootmaker, London house, Wharfage

Taylor George, surgery, Wharfage

—— John, mechanic, Wharfage

Thorn Alfred Henry, solicitor, Wharfage

Wall Richard, innkeeper, Roe Buck, High steet

Ward Beilby, greengrocer and furniture dealer, Madeley rd

—— Noah, stationer and newsagent, Tontine hill

Walton John, general smith, High st

**WATKISS THEOPHILUS, professor of music, Rodney bank**

**WATKISS THEOPHILUS, professor of music and organist at Broseley Parish Church, Rodney house, Coalbrookdale**

Webb Thomas Law, surgeon, South side

**WEBSTER JOHN HENRY, grocer, baker and provision merchant, Waterloo st**

**WESTWOOD Mrs., ladies' and children's outfitter, Wharfage**

White David, secretary of the Ironbridge Building Society, Madeley rd

—— D. H., insurance agent and rent and debt collector, Lincoln hill

——, foreman, Hodge bower

**WHITE JOSEPH WM., agent for the United Kingdom, Scottish Equitable, Shropshire and North Wales, and the Accidental Insurance Companies, Lloyd's bank**

**WILCOX B. and J., butchers and maltsters, High st**

Wilkinson John, salesman, Madeley rd

Wesleyan Mutual Improvement Society—Rev. R. Watkin Jones, president

Williams Ellen, grocer, poultry and flour dealer, Market sq

—— John, carter, Hodge bower

—— Lewis, tailor and woollen draper, Wharfage

**WILSON THOMAS BARNES, lic. victualler and brewer, Crown inn, Hodge bower**

**WILSON THOMAS BARNES, Tontine family and commercial Hotel, High st**

*

'Ironbridge, including Madeley Wood, is a market town on a steep acclivity; many of the houses, standing upon lofty precipices, have a picturesque appearance; it has a station on the railway, and is 6 miles south from Wellington, 6 south-west from Shifnal, 8 north-north-west from Bridgnorth and 13 east from Shrewsbury, and was formed into an ecclesiastical parish in 1845 from the parish of Madeley: . . . the name is derived from an iron bridge which crosses the Severn at this place; it was the first iron bridge of large dimensions constructed in this country and was cast and erected at Coalbrookdale in the years 1777–1779; the span of the arch is 100 feet, the width of the bridge, exclusive of parapets, is 26 feet, the height from the base line to the centre 40 feet, total weight of iron, 378 tons. The town is lighted by electricity and supplied with gas. The water supply is partly furnished by the Madeley and Broseley Water Company and partly derived from wells in the neighbourhood and is conveyed in iron mains to the town. The church of St. Luke, erected in 1837, is an edifice of brick, consisting of chancel, nave aisles and embattled tower, with pinnacles, containing a

clock and 8 tubular bells: the west window is stained: in 1920 a large marble tablet mounted on oak was erected in memory of the 42 men of Ironbridge who fell in the Great War, 1914–1918; . . . . The Methodist chapel, erected in the year 1837, is a structure of brick, and will hold about 700 persons; another Methodist chapel was erected in 1883, and will seat about 300. The Ironbridge Dispensary, in High Street, was established in 1828, but patients now attend the houses of the different surgeons; the average number of patients is about 1,000. The Police Station, on the Buildwas road, contains two cells and residence for inspector and two constables. The Madeley Institution, a structure of brick in the Gothic style, situated here, was erected in 1875 at a cost of £12,000. In the Market Square is a drinking fountain of red granite, erected in 1862 at the expense of Mrs Bartlett of Marnwood, in memory of her husband, the Rev. John Bartlett, M.A. The market day is on Friday and a fair is held annually on the 29th of May. The soil is principally clay, with a limestone bottom. Some wheat is grown here. The population in 1931 was 2,309.'

The Italian hill town of Ironbridge has its various levels connected by flights of brick steps. The longest, Church Steps (*far left*), provides the breathless with intermittent views first of chimneys and roofs and ultimately the river, the bridge and the woods beyond. At the top the steps have been encroached upon by the graveyard of St Luke's Church, which was extended eastwards across the steps in order to gain more space.

Mrs Longton's café is one of those vital but unappreciated visual elements of the Wharfage in Ironbridge, hanging on by the skin of its teeth until the imagination of the unseeing catches up— survival against the odds is a highly developed art in Ironbridge.

'Ironbridge . . . an uninteresting
and somewhat squalid town,
situated on a steep declivity sloping
down to the Severn, whose banks
are covered with slag and refuse!'
*J. E. Auden, 1912*

74

The public face which Ironbridge presents to the outside world of through-travellers or visitors standing on the bridge is composed of a series of brick house-fronts set in trees and spread up the south-facing slope of the Gorge. But once inside the town, the view is of tiled roofs and tall leaning chimneys suspended in front of a backdrop of trees, rising up from the edge of an invisible river, trees which are glamorously green in the summer, monochrome grey through the winter months. In both seasons the roofscape of Ironbridge is one of its great visual assets as deserving of priority attention as any window-frame or shop-front.

78

The sinisterly subliminal claim of
one of Britain's chief sign-makers
that 'the constant repetition of an
advertisement by enamelled iron
plates at station after station makes
an indelible impression on the
minds of visitors', was perhaps best
exemplified by those now extinct
blots of Stephens ink, although
cigarettes, cocoa and chocolate,
mustard, soap, metal polish and tea
were almost as penetrating in their
familiarity. So many of these signs
have now gone that at Coalport,
where they are still where they
ought to be, on the walls of
buildings, the effect is almost
startling.

Ironbridge is all paths and passageways, a continuous up and down progression of steps and tottering, leaning walls, each turn revealing a new dark hole in a wall or a breathtaking view to a horizon across the valley or three miles away. Crusty iron tie-plates and bars hold the place together, tree roots and the determined pressure of the soil pull it apart.

Nearly all the town is brick and tile with only a few of the bigger and older buildings roofed in slate, but the variety of colours and textures in the walls and copings, roofs and chimneys is infinite. For a start nothing is straight or horizontal. Brick courses follow the hill or they try an independent line approaching the level or more often they compromise and do neither. Everywhere vegetation crowds in.

Ironbridge has achieved a special sort of dereliction which has become almost a way of life. Often it is real, sometimes it is imagined, but always there is the feeling that it is there. It has provided reason and excuse for demolition and created appalling living conditions for many of the older inhabitants. It is picturesque and unhygienic, bizarre and appealing, as essential an element in the landscape of the Gorge as the Iron Bridge itself.

Waterloo Street is a museum of dereliction, systematically distorted with buildings carefully manicured to the point of collapse and then left standing. Sometimes a clue reveals life still going on behind the dead exterior: a dribble of cement dust from Beddoes' warehouse doors or the subtle polish around a hasp, staple and padlock which is discreetly used once or twice a week. But these are only gambits in the game of suspended animation that is Ironbridge.

Originally called Lincoln Hill House, South View dates from the 1830s, one of a range of large and in many cases distinguished houses built on the upper, south-facing slopes of the Gorge between the 1820s and 1880s. In this period Ironbridge developed into a prosperous and fashionable residential town.

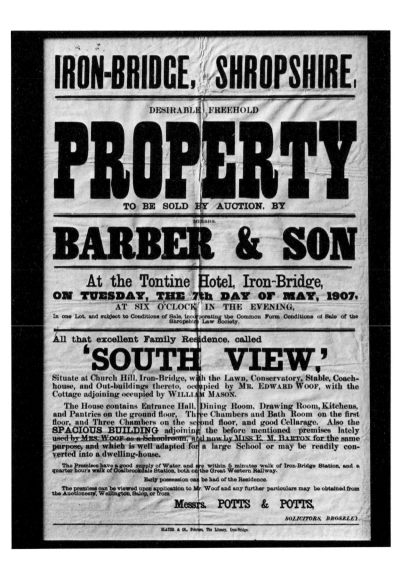

# IRON-BRIDGE, SHROPSHIRE,

DESIRABLE FREEHOLD

# PROPERTY

TO BE SOLD BY AUCTION, BY

MESSRS.

# BARBER & SON

At the Tontine Hotel, Iron-Bridge,
ON TUESDAY, THE 7th DAY OF MAY, 1907,
AT SIX O'CLOCK IN THE EVENING,

In one Lot, and subject to Conditions of Sale, incorporating the Common Form Conditions of Sale of the Shropshire Law Society.

All that excellent Family Residence, called

# 'SOUTH VIEW,'

Situate at Church Hill, Iron-Bridge, with the Lawn, Conservatory, Stable, Coachhouse, and Out-buildings thereto, occupied by MR. EDWARD WOOF, with the Cottage adjoining occupied by WILLIAM MASON.

The House contains Entrance Hall, Dining Room, Drawing Room, Kitchens, and Pantries on the ground floor, Three Chambers and Bath Room on the first floor, and Three Chambers on the second floor, and good Cellarage. Also the SPACIOUS BUILDING adjoining the before mentioned premises lately used by MRS. WOOF as a Schoolroom, and now by MISS E. M. BARTON for the same purpose, and which is well adapted for a large School or may be readily converted into a dwelling-house.

The Premises have a good supply of Water, and are within 5 minutes walk of Iron-Bridge Station, and a quarter hour's walk of Coalbrookdale Station, both on the Great Western Railway.

Early possession can be had of the Residence.

The premises can be viewed upon application to Mr. Woof and any further particulars may be obtained from the Auctioneers, Wellington, Salop, or from

Messrs. POTTS & POTTS,

SOLICITORS, BROSELEY.

SLATER & CO., Printers, The Library, Iron-Bridge.

Cast-iron and wrought-iron gates and railings in the Gorge to a great extent survived the depredations of the Second World War. Elsewhere miles of predominantly cast-iron railings were cut off, stacked at the foundries, but hardly used at all for the war effort. Cast-iron posts support wrought-iron gates in Woodside, Coalbrookdale.

The Coalbrookdale Company pioneered the large-scale use of cast-iron railings and offered a variety of ornamental designs in their late-nineteenth-century catalogues. In the Gorge relatively simple patterns predominate as in Coalbrookdale churchyard (*above*), and on the Iron Bridge (*below*).

Cheap and easily erected wrought-
iron railings found favour at the
turn of the century.

Quarrying and mining, subsidence and the throwing out of waste and ashes and slag, have created a man-made landscape of despoliation, a steeply broken and cratered terrain, much of which is now cloaked in hanging woodlands of close-packed broad-leaved trees. Every aspect of the natural landscape of the Gorge is wholly unnatural, the results of the colonization of the scars of clay-pits, the coppiced woods and the heaps of furnace slag and pit mounds. Oak and ash, invading sycamore, holly, rowan, beech, birch and hawthorn, are knotted with bramble, honeysuckle and ivy, iced over with old-man's-beard. Rosebay competes with wormwood for the few open clearings, or stands of gigantic foxgloves. Fallen trunks, thick in fungi, lie in rank, dank moss-covered rocks amongst the instant fossils of limestone wash from quarries, coating leaves and twigs. Orchids and nightingales, guelder rose, yellow archangel, foxes and badgers, wild garlic, clematis, stitchwort, lesser celandine, dog's mercury, enchanter's nightshade, wood sorrel, squirrels, spurge laurel and wood anemone, tree creepers and magpies.

A Victorian iron letter-box perches precariously in the wall of Church Hill, Ironbridge, supporting four different species of plant life.

'It is one arch, a hundred feet
broad, 52 high and 18 wide; all of
cast iron, weighing many hundred
tons. I doubt whether the Colossus
at Rhodes weighed much more.'

*John Wesley*, 1779

Progressive decline of the traditional commercial life of Ironbridge, which has been apparent for half a century or more, became critical in the early 1970s as new shopping centres, created as part of the new town of Telford, drew away shopkeepers to areas where prosperity was greater and there were more income-earners. This re-focusing of the shopping pattern has left Ironbridge high and dry but, paradoxically, the future of the town must be as an integral and fully functioning component of the New Town which is already creating the demand from people to live here, to occupy the empty houses and tend the overgrown gardens.

But the precise nature of Iron-bridge's role in Telford needs careful analysis if much of what the area represents today and, perhaps more important, has represented in the past, is not to be lost. A 'middle class enclave in South Telford' is not good enough, nor is 'dormitory of the New Town' sufficient for a town whose confidence and commercial strength as a self-contained community in its own right led to the setting up of the market here at the expense of well-established Madeley nearby. To shoe-horn new families with cars and children and twentieth-century wealth and aspirations into nineteenth-century artisans' dwellings on the one hand, and expect those dwellings to remain environmentally intact on the other, is to create unacceptable pressures on conservation strategies which in an area such as the Ironbridge Gorge are difficult to quantify and defend anyway. The answer must lie at a much more fundamental level, with the opportunities for publicly owned rental housing, special purpose housing associations and the conscious elimination at source of the pressures which cannot be realistically or even morally contained by manipulating existing conservation legislation.

Cast-iron grows out of the ground
in Coalbrookdale and Ironbridge,
sometimes anonymously to form a
discreet post of no known use at the
end of a wall, sometimes in
knobbed and fluted extravagance.

Two of the three lamp standards cast by the Coalbrookdale Company to commemorate Queen Victoria's Diamond Jubilee still stand, although only one, at Dale End, actually holds a light.

On Church Hill, Ironbridge, a cast-iron drinking fountain, almost certainly of non-local origin, has taken the fancy of the Department of the Environment and is now listed as architecturally and historically important.

The Iron Bridge, the first civil engineering work in the world constructed entirely of iron, is of unparalleled importance in the history of industry and technology, and as such has become recognized as one of the outstanding monuments to the adventurousness and skill of the eighteenth-century iron entrepreneurs. From its completion in 1781 the bridge was a spectacle and sight of wonderment, but after its survival of the great flood on the River Severn in February 1795, the only bridge on the whole course of the river to remain undamaged, it took on a new significance as an obvious progenitor of the new age of metal structures.

The project for a bridge had its origins in 1775 amongst a group of people interested in providing a connection across the river to link Coalbrookdale with the numerous mines, quarries and ironworks on the south side of the river. Amongst these partners was Abraham Darby III, John Wilkinson of Willey, one of the leading figures in the eighteenth-century iron trade, and a Shrewsbury architect called Thomas Farnolls Pritchard who at the first meeting was instructed to

prepare a design for a bridge. By the summer of 1777, after numerous changes of plan it was agreed that Darby should build a bridge of 90-foot span to the designs of Pritchard. In autumn 1777 however Pritchard died without a final design having been completed, and Darby was left with the job of building the bridge. Undoubtedly Darby had made a major contribution before the death of Pritchard and in view of the innovations which the bridge represented it would be natural to expect several people to be associated with it.

During 1778 the abutments providing the high-level approach for the bridge were completed and in the following year the enormous castings were made, the first two ribs, each weighing 5 tons 15 cwt, being lowered into place during July. By the autumn the main iron structure was complete; the expenditure of nine guineas on ale on 23 October probably celebrated the event.

Final completion was to take much longer however as the road approaches had still to be finished and the deck of the bridge surfaced, but on 1 January 1781 the opening took place. The bridge had cost in total £2,737 4s 4d, compared with the 1775 estimate of £550. Its method of assembly is of considerable interest in that joining techniques familiar to the carpenter

working in wood were used. Halved
dovetails with pegs fastened the
radial members to the main ribs
whilst mortise joints held by wedges
were used to secure the ribs
themselves to the vertical and
horizontal members at each end.
Over the years the ropes used for
handling sailing barges have cut
deeply into the iron ribs of the
bridge. The weight of iron in the
bridge is 378 tons 10 cwt, which for
a span of 100 feet 6 inches was
substantially more than was used
again in bridges of similar
dimensions. This illustrates the
unfamiliarity of the bridge's
builders with the structural use of
cast iron and an understandable
concession to caution.

Completion of the bridge led to a
reorganization of the road pattern
of the surrounding area and the
almost immediate and very rapid
growth of the town of Ironbridge
on the south-facing slope of the
Gorge. Initially only the road now
called the Wharfage provided a link
on the north side, but the bridge
proprietors built a new route, now
named Church Hill, to provide a
connection with the Madeley
turnpike at the top of Lincoln Hill.
On the south side they built the
road still called Bridge Road to
link with the Broseley to Much
Wenlock turnpike.

By October 1781 the Shrewsbury to
London stage coach 'The Diligence'
was using the bridge, whilst shortly
afterwards the Madeley market was
transferred to a site at the north end

of the bridge where it is still held every Friday. During the twenty years after 1781 the market-place became the focal point of a thriving little town which by the 1830s contained a variety of commercial and professional concerns.

Soon after its completion it was realized that the bridge was in trouble as the result of movement of the stone abutments. Various remedial works were carried out culminating in the insertion of the two iron side arches in the north abutment which are there today. Although this undoubtedly helped, movement on the other side continued until in 1931 with increased traffic loads becoming an added problem it was closed to all but pedestrians. Vehicular traffic then all had to cross the Severn by the 'Free Bridge', a reinforced concrete structure built half a mile downstream opened in 1909. In 1950 the bridge trustees handed the Iron Bridge over to Salop County Council and the tolls were abolished, but it was not until 1972, largely with funds raised by the Ironbridge Gorge Museum Trust, that the first stage of the long-awaited strengthening work could begin. The structural parts of this restoration programme are now complete so that today the two sides of the bridge are held in constant relationship to each other by a reinforced concrete slab in the bed of the river between the two abutments.

In a hut by the Severn, a few yards downstream from the Iron Bridge, is England's only coracle-maker. Mr Eustace Rogers still makes the peculiar Ironbridge variant of the River Severn coracle, which owes much of its design to the needs of poaching and rabbit-catching. Less clumsy than the coracles favoured by salmon fishers, some stability has been sacrificed to speed and manoeuvrability and as a result the design, developed over generations by the Rogers, father and son, has become established in the form of a shallow oval bowl, the two ends equally rounded.

The framework consists of sawn ash laths or 'splints'. Typically, they form fore-and-aft frames with nine interlaced at right angles but the numbers are not standardized and relate closely to the height and weight of the man for whom the coracle is made. The gunwales, of lath bands or hoops, support a nine-inch board as a seat, and the whole is covered in unbleached calico coated with a mixture of tar and pitch. On dry land the coracle man looks like a giant beetle, the great black wing case hung across his shoulders on the end of the paddle, but still light enough for him to walk ten miles across country if need be. Once in the water he becomes nimble; with casual wrist-flicking figure-of-eight movements of the wooden shovel over the bows the walnut shell skims and twists, an optical illusion.

Eustace works part of his life in the power station, but the Iron Bridge and the Industrial Revolution were only a brief interlude hardly referred to when he talks of gin-traps and poaching, of hauling bodies from the river, of the underwater geography of the Severn as clear to him as if there were no water.

Steep gradients and tight curves lead the railway into the head of Coalbrookdale.

The Great Western station at Coalport survives surprisingly intact since its closure in 1963.

By the time of the railway revolution in the 1840s the Ironbridge Gorge was already of declining importance and lay geographically and technically outside the mainstream of the nation's industrial development. As a result, railways came late to the area and although Lightmoor, to the north of the Gorge, had a railway link with the main Shrewsbury, Wellington, Wolverhampton line by 1854 it was not until 1857 that Coalbrookdale itself had a rail connection. This line was operated by the Coalbrookdale Company until 1861 and eventually became part of the network of lines operated by the Great Western Railway in the area.

The Great Western did not have the territory to itself, however, for in 1861 the London and North-Western Railway opened a branch line from Hadley on their Wellington to Stafford line, through Oakengates and Dawley to a

terminus beside the River Severn at Coalport. Although originally conceived as part of a larger scheme to invade south Shropshire nothing ever came of these proposals and the line remained an isolated arm of the L. & N.W.R. in an area otherwise dominated by the Great Western. Passenger services were withdrawn in 1954 and the line closed south of Dawley in 1960 and completely in 1964.

The Great Western's presence in the Gorge itself was established in 1862 when the Severn Valley Railway was opened, closely following the river for nearly forty miles from Hartlebury on the Oxford, Worcester and Wolverhampton Railway to a junction with the Shrewsbury and Hereford Railway at Sutton Bridge, a mile south of Shrewsbury. At the outset the line was operated by the G.W.R. with which it amalgamated ten years later. Traffic was never very heavy and a service of four passenger trains a day in each direction remained standard for many years before the line was closed in 1963.

Opening on the same day as the Severn Valley Railway and forming a junction with it at Buildwas was the Much Wenlock and Severn Junction Railway, operated by the G.W.R. and initially consisting merely of a $3\frac{1}{2}$-mile branch to Much Wenlock. Later the Much Wenlock, Craven

Arms and Coalbrookdale Railway Company, incorporated in 1861, extended this branch south-westwards, but, more important to the railway network of the Gorge, also made the link northwards into Coalbrookdale and an end-on link with the existing branch. The River Severn was crossed on a cast-iron arched bridge of single span, the Albert Edward Bridge, opened in 1864. This line, with the bridge, is now the only railway still operating in the area, carrying coal and oil to the two Ironbridge power stations.

Remains of the Severn Valley Railway through Coalport and Jackfield are numerous, with Coalport station (*facing page*) still virtually complete and level crossing gates *in situ* at Jackfield. In Ironbridge the station site is now a car park.

Brick walls define boundaries and maintain privacy in Ironbridge and Coalbrookdale, less so elsewhere. Indeed the wallscape of the area is one of its outstanding features, making ordinary paths and steps into canyons, leaning and tottering with the movements of the hillsides, crumbling from lack of proper maintenance. Idiosyncratic brick courses, sometimes running with the slope, often not, make the problems of their retention difficult, but it is essential that they should stay.

The great Hay inclined plane was built in the early 1790s to link the upper sections of the Shropshire Canal system running northwards to Oakengates and Wrockwardine Wood with Coalport Basin, the point where goods could be transferred to the sailing barges on the River Severn for shipment downstream to Stourport and Bristol. It is the most spectacular surviving monument of the tub-boat canal system which embraced the whole Shropshire coalfield and provided transport for what was then Britain's most prolific iron-producing area. As a system the Shropshire Canal was highly successful, particularly in view of the nature of the terrain on the high plateau of the coalfield, but a large part of its success lay in the use of inclined planes which ensured the rapid movement of boats between levels without the enormous consumption of water incurred by conventional flights of locks. Of the six inclines employed on the coalfield the Hay was the largest with a vertical rise of 207 feet in a horizontal distance of about 1000 feet. It was equivalent to twenty-seven locks, but was worked by only four men who could pass a pair of six-ton tub boats over it in less than four minutes; the equivalent locks would have involved some two or three hours.

The sequence of operation involved boats at the upper and lower basins entering submerged cradles to which they were attached by chains. The prevailing direction of traffic was downhill, towards the river, so as the loaded boat descended it could haul up the empty boat in its cradle from the foot of the incline. A steam engine was installed at the upper basin to winch the cradle over the lip of the canal before it started its descent; this engine could also, on occasion, lift a loaded boat up the incline.

By the 1860s much of the Shropshire Canal had been severely damaged by mining subsidence and increasing railway competition was substantially reducing its traffic. The incline was last used in 1894, the rails were removed in 1910 and the area rapidly turned into wilderness. Since 1968, however, the incline has been cleared by the Ironbridge Gorge Museum Trust, the upper and lower basins reinstated and the track replaced.

Obvious surface remains of the mining industry in the Ironbridge Gorge are now rare and the examples shown here are actively preserved in the Blists Hill Open Air Museum where a steam engine from a local clay-pit is in regular use winding a cage in a restored shaft. Underground, however, the sides of the Gorge are honeycombed with tunnels and adits, used mainly for the extraction of limestone and iron ore.

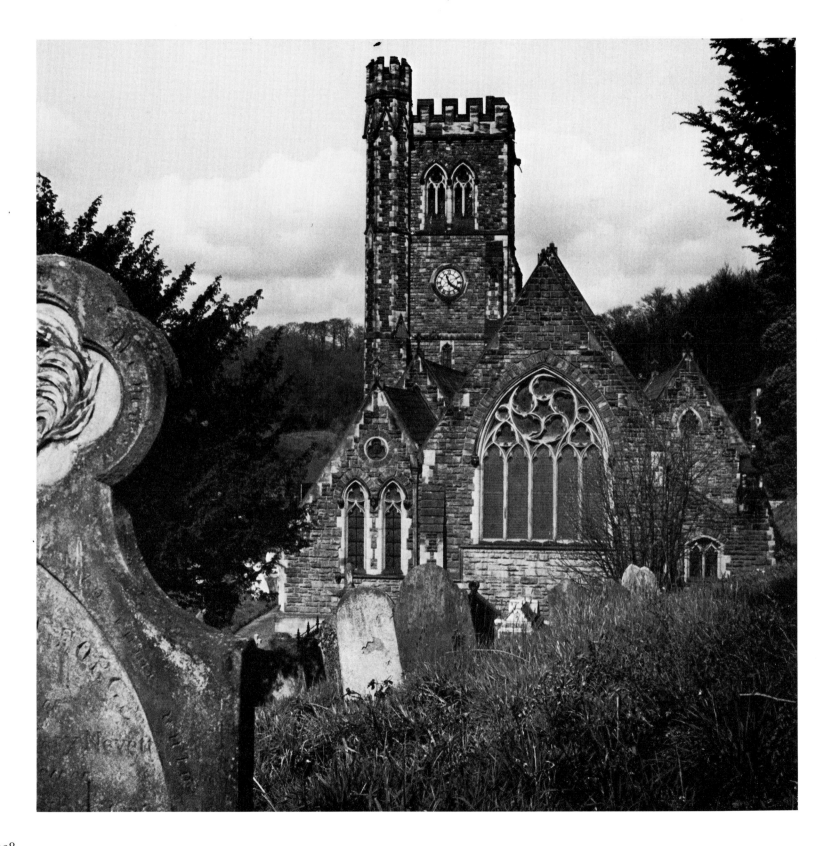

Abraham Darby IV turned away from Quakerism to the Church of England and in the early 1850s commissioned the London architects, Reeves and Butcher, to design a new Anglican church, for which he paid, and which was consecrated in 1854. The plan consists of a chancel and nave with side aisles and the tower at the south-west corner. Holy Trinity contains a number of products from the Coalbrookdale Company across the road, including cast-iron openwork in the pew doors. Iron grave-marker plates abound in the churchyard.

The spontaneous rise of Ironbridge as a new community independent of nearby Coalbrookdale came about rapidly after the construction of the bridge, with the Tontine Hotel completed in two stages by 1786 and the market building and bank in the 1790s. Church Hill, the original road from the bridge, was rapidly developed after about 1820 and by the 1830s the new town, already boasting its new name of Iron-Bridge, could support an Anglican church, built of Madeley Wood Company bricks at a total cost of £3232 and consecrated in 1837.

'The church, a handsome structure of brick, dedicated to St. Luke, is situated on elevated ground, and approached by a flight of steps one hundred and nineteen in number. It was built in the year 1836, and consists of nave, chancel, and side aisles, with a tower, in which is one bell. The east window is richly beautified with stained glass, and has full-length figures of St. Peter, St. James and St. John, executed by the celebrated Evans of Shrewsbury.'

Samuel Bagshaw, *History, Gazetteer, and Directory of Shropshire*, 1851

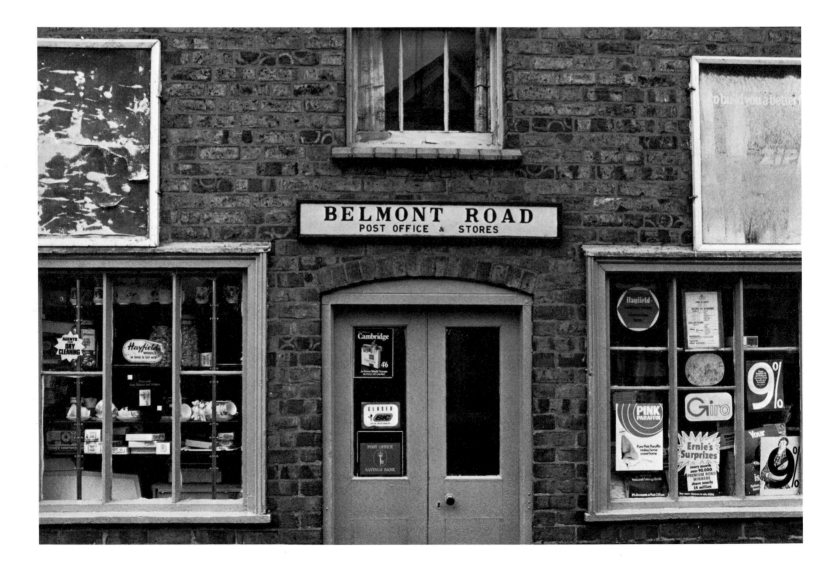

Jockey Bank, a hillside community in its own right, perched above Madeley Wood, is gradually losing its grip on the hillside. Here some of the worst effects of decay have been felt with derelict houses and in some cases unstable ground. In 1935 a landslide in the area destroyed part of the town. But Jockey Bank is a necessary component of the local scene, prominent from many parts of the lower Gorge and an *hors d'oeuvre* essential to the experience of the river and its environs below. More important, people want to live there.

The Wesleyan School, Madeley
Wood, opened on 3 January 1859.

TO THE
MEMORY OF THE
REV JOHN W^m FLETCHER
TWENTYFIVE YEARS VICAR
OF THIS PARISH
A MAN OF APOSTOLICAL
PIETY AND ZEAL
WHO IN THE DISCHARGE OF
HIS
EXEMPLARY MINISTRY
CARED WITH SINGULAR
APPLICATION
FOR THE SCRIPTURAL
EDUCATION
OF HIS YOUNG
PARISHIONERS
AND IN
PURSUANCE OF THAT
OBJECT
PROVIDED THE ADJACENT
SCHOOLROOM
THUS PREPARING THE WAY
FOR
A COURSE OF TRAINING
WHICH HAS CONTINUED
TO THE PRESENT TIME
THESE NEW BUILDINGS
ARE INSCRIBED

M D C C C L V I I I

135

On the south side of the valley, brooding across the Severn towards the Coalport inclined plane, stands the Tuckies, an isolated, ancient and decrepit house which in 1787 was leased by Archibald Cochrane, ninth Earl Dundonald. From here he supervised the affairs of the British Tar Company, a financially unsuccessful concern set up on the riverside to distil tar from coal under the terms of a patent taken out in 1781.

Today the house and neighbouring farm, more than anywhere else in the whole Gorge, exude a surrealistic atmosphere of remoteness from the world and of time having stood still.

The emergence of the prosperous middle classes and the growth of a consumer market, board schools and nonconformist chapels, the popular pursuit of *Art* and *Beauty*, and machinery designed not to save labour so much as increase production, provided a foundation stone for the manufacture in colossal quantities of wall and floor tiles. Amongst the tangible visual symbols of Victorianism the glazed or encaustic tile comes high on the list, and even after nearly half a century of being desperately out of fashion it can still be seen, chipped in the dado of a seedy pub, forming decorative panels in a cast-iron fire grate or setting the scene for the hydraulic ritual of some subterranean lavatory.

Many of these tiles come from the Gorge where in the 1840s high-quality tile clay deposits were discovered and where in 1852 the firm of Maw became established, initially at Benthall near Ironbridge. By the 1880s this first site had become too cramped and a new 'Benthall Works' was set up at Jackfield, downstream from Ironbridge and near another tile manufacturer, Craven Dunnill, who had started there in 1875. By the end of the nineteenth century Maw's were the largest tile producers in the world, making glazed tiles for walls and decorative panels and encaustic tiles for floors. These latter were pressed from plastic clay of the consistency of plasticine into which a pattern was impressed and filled with liquid clay of a different colour. Designs were largely produced by the firm's own staff of designers, but well-known architects such as Alfred Waterhouse and George Edward Street were also commissioned. George Maw's own interest in geology and botany—he was a Fellow of the Linnaean Society—undoubtedly affected his attitude to design, whilst Craven Dunnill specialized in well-researched reproductions of medieval floor tiles in browns and creams.

By the 1930s the tile industry was in decline but although Craven Dunnills closed in 1952, Maw's hung on until 1969 before production finally ceased. Craven Dunnill's works is occupied by an iron foundry, but Maw's enormous premises lie empty, cocooned and awaiting some new and sympathetic user. The Ironbridge Gorge Museum has several thousand tiles from the two companies, but their real memorials are in the Mysore Palace and the University of Toronto, the pubs of Birmingham and the London Underground.

One of the lesser-known bridges of the Ironbridge Gorge is Lee Dingle Bridge, built in the 1860s to carry a tramway from coalpits to Blists Hill blast furnaces. Long out of use, its skeletal remains are now within the area of Blists Hill Open Air Museum, the ends guarded by ostentatious approaches, its own cast-iron gravestones.

'Jackfield, an ecclesiastical parish formed February 7 1862, is 1 mile north-east from the town of Broseley, 1 east-by-south from Ironbridge station and 1 north-west from Coalport, on the Severn Valley line, and on the bank of the river Severn, which separates it from Madeley.'

'The new church of St Mary, erected in 1863, as a memorial to G. Pritchard Esq. late high sheriff of Salop, at a cost of £3,000, is in the French Pointed style of coloured bricks with stone dressings, and is cruciform, from designs by Sir A. W. Blomfield, A.R.A., F.S.A.: it is sited on the side of the river between the railway and the Severn: the church has a north porch and a turret 75 feet high, containing one bell: there are 300 sittings.'

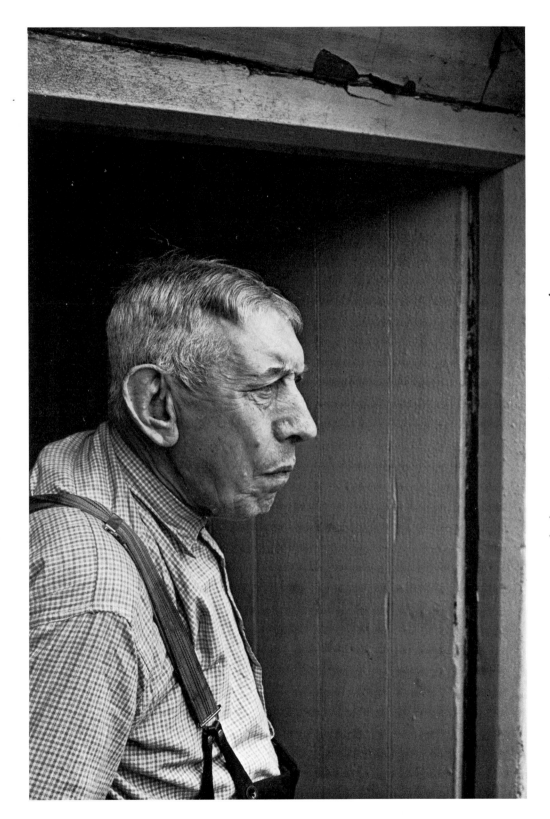

John Bradley of Jackfield died at the age of eighty on 7 March 1975. He was born in the Mount Pleasant cottage where he spent the whole of his life, one of a row of cottages which local legend suggests were built by Dutch immigrants connected with the boat trade on the river. Several have roof beams which may have been the masts of sailing barges. Everybody here had some connection with the river, and John Bradley's grandfather ran the Jane Shore ferry at the Tuckies long before the Jackfield and Coalport memorial footbridge was built.

Mr Bradley's first job after leaving school was as telegraph boy at Jackfield post office; later he worked a tile press in Maw's tileries and had a brief spell of war work at Donnington ordnance depot in the 1940s before returning to Maw's. For many years he was a member of the committee of Jackfield Silver Band and at one stage was Vice-Chairman.

Electricity never came to Mount Pleasant, but gas lighting did and the kettle was always on the sway over the fire. John Bradley's home was warm and clean. On the sideboard were Staffordshire dogs and cow creamers and on either side photographs, of the silver band and himself as a young man on the left, of his mother on the right. John's trilby hat always hung on the frame of his mother's photograph, his cap on a hook to the right of the fire.

John Bradley's generation knew Coalbrookdale, Ironbridge, Jackfield and Coalport as prosperous happy places, not perhaps as busy as in earlier years but bustling and full of social life, close-knit industrious communities by the river.

Coalport Bridge marks the downstream or eastern end of the industrial section of the Severn valley and effectively of the Gorge itself. Its history is complex and only confused by the date 1818 on the ornamental centre panel.

Anxious to improve communications across this lower section of the Gorge, a group of subscribers, including notable local ironmasters such as John Wilkinson and Daniel Onions, petitioned Parliament for an Act to build a bridge between Preens Eddy in the parish of Broseley on the south side of the river and the Sheepwash on the borders of Madeley and Sutton Maddock on the north. At the same time the Iron Bridge project was being actively promoted and obtained its Act in 1776. The Iron Bridge subscribers agreed not to offer opposition to the new bridge at Preens Eddy and its Act was passed in 1777.

The bridge as built had two spans with a central stone pier and was called the Wood Bridge although the wooden arch and supporting structure were in fact supported on iron ribs. In the early nineteenth century the bridge was replaced by the present Coalport bridge which may conceivably incorporate pieces from the original. What is almost certain is that both the first bridges in the Gorge were made of iron or used it in their construction.

The Coalport china works was an isolated but important centre of a trade which had its traditional seat in Staffordshire. The origins of pottery manufacture on this Severnside site are obscure, but by the late eighteenth century it was well established and soon after 1814 when John Rose purchased the site, over 400 people were employed there. The factory remained a large one and by the 1850s had some 500 employees, but despite the fact that it enjoyed many of the natural advantages and traditions of the Staffordshire-based industry, and its wares were fine and well thought of, it remained outside the mainstream of the industry. After the First World War the company had a succession of difficulties which culminated in a move to Stoke-on-Trent in 1926 where Coalport china is still made. The china works site has had a variety of uses since then, but two bottle kilns remain externally complete and a third has been cut down in height for reasons of safety. The works are now in the hands of the Ironbridge Gorge Museum Trust and form the basis of a museum of the ceramics industry.

Ironbridge, separated pieces, a roof, a sky, a chimney; you have seen each one before. It is only when they come together, first in small groups and finally linked within the border of the puzzle, that the whole picture emerges.

# Index

Attingham Hall, 14

Beddoes' warehouse, Ironbridge, 84
Bedlam blast furnaces, 13, 16, 19
Benthall Works, 141
Blists Hill, 16, 18, 125, 145
Bradley, John, 148–53

Café, Mrs Longton's, Ironbridge, 72
Carpenters' Row, 15, 19, 40, 41
'Chestnuts, The', 14
Church Hill, 99, 107, 109, 111, 130, 131
Church Row, 15
Church Steps, 71
Coalbrookdale, 10–20; Old Furnace at, 14, 21, 48, 49; described, 1851, 28; Darby Furnace Site at, 23, 35; railway at, 35; Tea Kettle Row, 36; described, 1758, 38, 39: Holy Trinity, 43; Literary and Scientific Institute, 15, 46; The Grange, coach house at, 48, 52, 53; Upper Furnace Pool, 15, 48; Quaker Burial Ground at, 50, 52, 53; Wesleyan Chapel at, 55; Woodside, 90
Coalbrookdale Company, 12, 13, 14, 17; builds Great Warehouse, 24; catalogues of, 31, 32, 33; builds Carpenters' Row, 40, 41; wharf for, 58; builds warehouse, 58; and cast-iron railings, 92, 93; casts lamp standards, 106, 107; makes church furniture, 126
Coalport, 16, 76, 77, 79, 119, 155, 156
Craven Dunnill, tile manufacturers, 17, 141

Dale End, Coalbrookdale, 15, 16, 17, 57, 107
'Dale House', 14
Darby family, 12–15, 23–4, 48, 50, 52, 53, 109, 110, 111, 112, 129
Darby Furnace site, 23, 24, 34, 35
Donnington Wood; ironworks, 13; Shropshire Canal at, 16

Engine Row, 15

Furnaces, 14, 23, 24, 35, 48, 145

Gothic warehouse, 58
'Grange, The', Coalbrookdale, 14, 15, 48
Great Britain, S.S., 14
Great Warehouse, the, 15, 24

Hay inclined plane, 124, 125, 139
Holy Trinity Church, Coalbrookdale, 42, 43, 129
Horsehay works, 13, 14

Institute, Literary and Scientific, Coalbrookdale, 46
Iron Bridge, the, 13, 62, 68–9, 92, 93, 102, 103, 109–12, 116
Ironbridge: power stations, 57; St Luke's Church, 56; Methodist chapels, 57; Church Steps, 71; Waterloo Street, 84; Beddoes' Warehouse at, 84; 'South View', 88, 89; Church Hill, 99, 106, 107; Tontine Hotel, 130, 131; described, 1851, 130, 131; coracle-maker at, 116, 117; church described, 1851, 130, 131
'Ironbridge Commercial Directory', 62–7
Ironbridge Gorge Museum Trust, 7, 18, 23, 40, 41, 48, 111, 112, 124, 125, 141, 156

Jackfield, 141, 146, 148
Jockey Bank, 134

Lee Dingle Bridge, 145
Loadcroft Wharf, 58

Madeley, 68, 69; Court, 14
Madeley Wood Ironworks, 14
Maw's, tile manufacturers, 16, 17, 141, 148

Old Furnace, Coalbrookdale, 23

Pritchard, Thomas Farnolls, 109, 110, 112, 113

Quaker Burial Ground, Coalbrookdale, 14, 50, 51, 52, 53

Reynolds, Richard, 13, 14
Reynolds, William, 14, 16

Rogers, Eustace, coracle-maker, 116
Rose Cottages, 15, 19

Snapper Furnace, 23
St Luke's Church, Ironbridge, 71
St Mary's Church, Jackfield, 146
'South View', Ironbridge, 88, 89

Tea Kettle Row, 15, 36
Telford New Town, 17, 20, 36, 102–3
Tontine Hotel, 130, 131
'Tuckies', 139, 148

Upper Furnace Pool, 14, 15, 48

War memorials: Coalbrookdale, 46; Ironbridge, 69
Waterloo Street, Ironbridge, 84
Wesleyan Chapel, Coalbrookdale, 15, 55
Wharfage, The, 62, 72, 109, 111
Wilkinson, John, 13, 109, 155
Wood Bridge, 155
Woodside, Coalbrookdale, 90

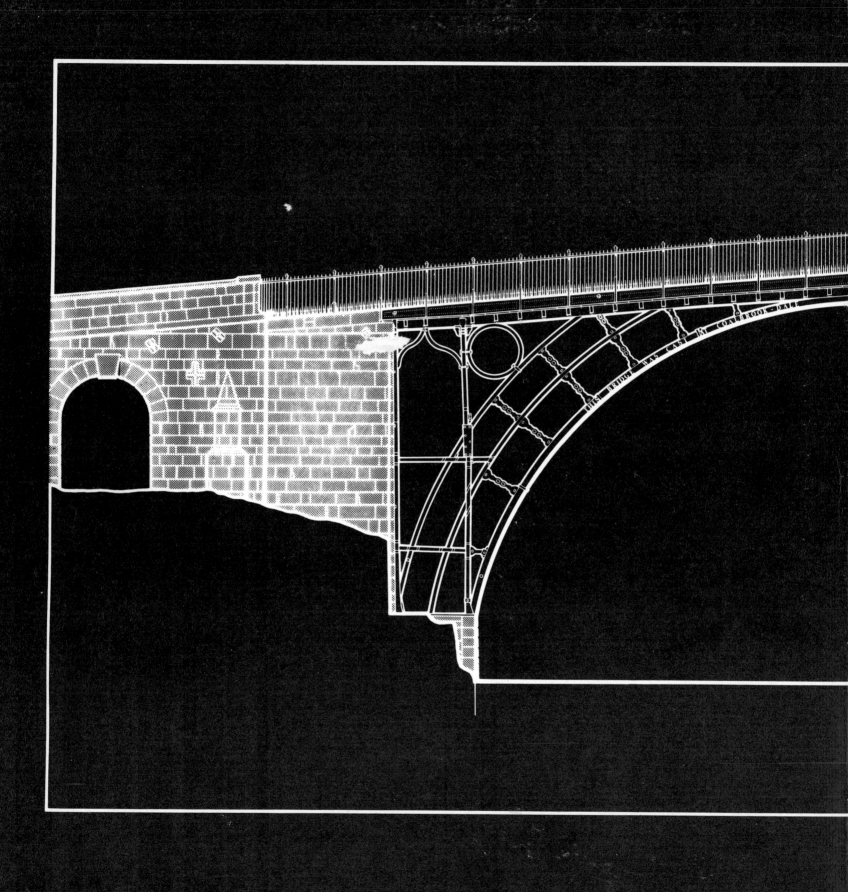